W0346617

STARK

KOMPAKT-WISSEN
ENGLISCH

Rainer Jacob

Themenwortschatz

Hauptschule

STARK

ISBN 978-3-89449-878-8

www.stark-verlag.de
1. Auflage 2006

Inhalt

Vorwort

Liebe Schülerin, lieber Schüler,

du hast sicher schon gemerkt, wie wichtig Vokabeln im Englischunterricht sind. Egal, ob es darum geht, einen Text richtig zu verstehen, Fragen zu beantworten, einen Brief oder sonstigen Text zu verfassen – immer brauchst du einen umfangreichen Wortschatz. Damit du sicher und gut gerüstet in Klassenarbeiten und in deine Hauptschulabschlussprüfung gehen kannst, bietet dir dieser Band doppelte Hilfe an.

- Zum einen sind die Vokabeln zu den wichtigsten Themen, die im Unterricht behandelt werden, übersichtlich in einzelnen Kapiteln zusammengestellt. Auf diese Weise lassen sie sich leichter lernen. Außer der deutschen Bedeutung des Wortes findest du auch einen Beispielsatz: Erst durch die Verwendung des Wortes in einem sinnvollen Zusammenhang wird dir klar, wie du das Wort anwenden kannst. Hier kannst du auch Synonyme (Wörter, die dieselbe Bedeutung haben) und Antonyme (Wörter, die die entgegengesetzte Bedeutung haben) nachsehen.

- Zum anderen enthält unser Themenwortschatz einen umfangreichen Nachschlageteil mit dem Grundwortschatz für die Hauptschule. Dort kannst du alle Wörter, die du (noch) nicht kennst, nachschlagen, um sie dann zu lernen und in deinen Wortschatz aufzunehmen.

Viel Erfolg für deine Klassenarbeiten und die Hauptschulabschlussprüfung!

Rainer Jacob

Abkürzungsverzeichnis

AE	American English
BE	British English
a.m.	vormittags
p.m.	nachmittags
etw.	etwas
jmdm.	jemandem
jmdn.	jemanden
Pl.	Plural
=	Synonym (Wort mit gleicher Bedeutung)
≠	Antonym (Wort mit entgegengesetzter Bedeutung)
[ɪ]	Lautschrift, die erklärt, wie ein Wort ausgesprochen wird

Family and Friends

vocabulary	dt. Bedeutung	English sentence	syn/opp
acquaintance	*Bekanntschaft*	I don't know Alan very well, he is just an acquaintance.	
adult	*erwachsen* *Erwachsene(r)*	More young girls than adult women go on a diet.	= grown-up ≠ youngster
ancestor	*Vorfahr(e)*	Ali's ancestors came to England from Pakistan.	= forefather
aunt	*Tante*	My aunt Zoe is the sister of my mother.	
birth by birth	*Geburt* *von Geburt*	Mohammed is Pakistani by birth.	
(to) give birth	*zur Welt bringen*	Barbara gave birth to four children.	= (to) bear a child
birthday	*Geburtstag*	When is your birthday?	
boyfriend	*Freund*	Most girls in my class have a steady ("festen") boyfriend.	
breadwinner	*Brotverdiener*	My father has lost his job; that is why my mother is the breadwinner.	
(to) bring up	*jmdn. aufziehen, erziehen*	Marc was brought up by his grandfather.	= (to) educate
brother	*Bruder*	Sue has got two brothers, Simon and Luke.	≠ sister
child	*Kind*	As a child I was always taller than everyone else in my class.	≠ grown-up, adult
company	*Gesellschaft*	Kevin's mother thinks that some of his friends are bad company.	

vocabulary	dt. Bedeutung	English sentence	syn/opp
cousin	*Cousin, Cousine*	I'd like you to meet my cousin Linda.	
date of birth	*Geburtsdatum*	My sister's date of birth is 3 January 1995.	
daughter	*Tochter*	The Millers have five children – two daughters and three sons.	≠ son
elder	*ältere(r)*	Laura is the daughter of my elder brother James.	≠ younger
engaged engagement	*verlobt* *Verlobung*	Last Christmas my sister became engaged to Michael Davies.	
family member	*Familienan-gehörige(r)*	At my grandfather's 65th birthday all the family members came together.	
father	*Vater*	I told my father I wanted to become an astronaut.	
female	*weiblich*	There are more female workers in industry today.	≠ male
first name	*Vorname*	Three girls in my class have the same first name: Amy.	≠ surname
foster child	*Pflegekind*	a child who is taken care of by a couple who are not his/her natural parents	
friend (to) make friends (to) become friends	*Freund* *Freundschaft schließen* *Freunde werden*	Captain John Smith and the Indian chief became friends.	≠ enemy
friendly	*freundlich*	Charles Frost had a friendly look in his eye.	≠ unfriendly
friendship	*Freundschaft*	I hope my friendship to Tom will last for ever.	

vocabulary	dt. Bedeutung	English sentence	syn/opp
girlfriend	*Freundin*	Have you heard that Chris has got a new girlfriend?	
grandchild	*Enkel (-kind)*	Our neighbour, Mr Myers, has twelve grandchildren.	
grandfather	*Großvater*	My grandfather had to walk six kilometres to school every day.	
grandmother	*Großmutter*	My grandmother showed my mother how to make a Christmas pudding.	
grandparents	*Großeltern*	When I can't get what I want from my mother, I always ask my grandparents.	
grown-up	*Erwachsener*	Cinema tickets for children are cheaper than tickets for grown-ups.	= adult ≠ kid, youngster
human human being	*menschlich* *Mensch*	To err ("irren") is human. All human beings should have the same rights.	≠ inhuman = man
husband	*Ehemann*	Mrs Miller's husband works as a mechanic.	
kid	*Kind, Jugendliche(r)*	A new kid from Ireland came into our class.	= youngster ≠ grown-up, adult
lonely loneliness	*einsam* *Einsamkeit*	Parents think that their children are lonely when they play with their computers all day.	
(to) marry	*heiraten*	Sue said she would only marry for love, not for money.	
member	*Mitglied*	I'm a member of our local football club.	

vocabulary	dt. Bedeutung	English sentence	syn/opp
membership	*Mitgliedschaft*	The membership in our local football club is going down.	
mother	*Mutter*	My mother was only twenty years old when I was born.	
neighbour	*Nachbar*	We often help our neighbours and they help us.	
parents	*Eltern*	Parents want their children to have a good education.	
place of birth	*Geburtsort*	A passport shows your name and place of birth.	
population	*Bevölkerung*	Great Britain has a population of about 60 million people.	
relative	*Verwandter*	On Sundays we visit our relatives.	
related	*verwandt*	I'm not related to Harry although we both have the same family name.	
(to) separate	*sich trennen*	After seven years of living together Brad and Nicole separated.	
single	*ledig*	Today girls do not marry young; they remain single longer.	≠ married
single mother	*alleinerziehende Mutter*	Sophie is a single mother and works in a super-market.	
single parent	*Allein-erziehende(r)*	a person who looks after their child or children without a husband or wife	
sister	*Schwester*	My sister likes music and ballet.	≠ brother

vocabulary	dt. Bedeutung	English sentence	syn/opp
son	*Sohn*	Shail is the son of Indian immigrants.	≠ daughter
(to) start a family	*eine Familie gründen*	Jane and Leo started a family when they were still teenagers.	
stepfather stepson	*Stiefvater* *Stiefsohn*	Brian's mother married again. Her new husband is Brian's stepfather.	
stepmother stepdaughter	*Stiefmutter* *Stieftochter*	In one of the stories of the Brothers Grimm a stepmother tries to kill her stepdaughter.	
(to) support	*unterstützen*	My Mum and my Dad help me as much as they can; they support me.	
(to) support a family	*eine Familie ernähren*	If you earn money you can support a family.	
surname	*Nachname*	My first name is Jeff and my surname is Mills.	≠ first name
twin	*Zwilling*	Louise and Jemma are twins; they look very much alike.	
uncle	*Onkel*	My uncle is a doctor at a hospital in Cork.	≠ aunt
wife	*Ehefrau*	Pete met his wife Karin when he worked in Germany.	≠ husband
youngster	*Jugendlicher*	David Attenborough became interested in animals as a youngster.	
youth	*Jugendlicher; Jugend*	Many black youths love playing basketball.	≠ adult

School

vocabulary	dt. Bedeutung	English sentence	syn/opp
at school	*in der Schule*	Did you have a good day at school?	
(to) be good at	*gut sein in*	Eric is very good at sport – he is our best footballer.	
bullying	*Tyrannisieren, Ärgern, Einschüchtern von Mitschülern*	Bullying makes life at school very difficult for boys and girls.	
bully	*Tyrann, gemeiner Mitschüler*	Barry was one of the worst bullies at my school.	
career	*berufliche Laufbahn, Karriere*	Julie dreams of a career as a fashion model.	
charge	*Verantwortung*		
(to) be in charge of	*verantwortlich sein für, Verantwortung tragen*	A headmaster is in charge of a school.	
(to) choose	*wählen*	In the USA pupils can choose some of their school subjects.	
choice	*Auswahl*	Taking up French instead of Latin was a good choice.	
(to) copy	*abschreiben, kopieren*	Use your own words. Do not copy from the text.	
course	*Kurs*	Bill Gates left university without finishing his course.	
(to) correct	*korrigieren*	Teachers say they spend more time correcting than teaching.	= (to) mark
correction	*Korrektur*		
day out	*(Tages-) Ausflug*	Last Tuesday we had a day out at the zoo.	= school trip, excursion

vocabulary	dt. Bedeutung	English sentence	syn/opp
detention	*Nachsitzen*	I had to go to detention because I had been late for school three times.	
(to) do home-work	*Hausaufgaben machen*	Simon always does his homework before he watches TV.	
(to) do well	*gut abschneiden*	Students work hard to do well in their tests.	
drama group	*Theatergruppe, Theatertruppe*	I have been a member of our drama group for three years.	
(to) drop out of school	*die Schule abbrechen, vorzeitig verlassen*	Jake dropped out of school and started working at a supermarket.	
education	*Ausbildung, Bildung*	Parents want their children to have a good education.	
effect	*Wirkung, Auswirkung*	Pupils know that exams have a big effect on their future.	
(to) enter	*eintreten*	In 1995 Prince William entered the exclusive Eton College.	
exam	*Prüfung*	May, June and July are the main months for exams at English schools.	= test
exchange programme	*Austausch-programm*	Every year hundreds of young people spend a year in the United States.	
excursion	*Ausflug, Exkursion*	The class went on an excursion to Windsor Castle.	= school trip
exercise book	*Heft*	Open your exercise books, please.	

vocabulary	dt. Bedeutung	English sentence	syn/opp
extra classes	*Nachhilfe*	Irene has extra classes in maths.	
(to) fail	*nicht bestehen, durchfallen*	If an American student fails a number of subjects, he does not have to stay at school for an extra year.	
(to) finish school	*die Schule beenden*	As soon as I finish school I want to work.	
foreign language	*Fremdsprache*	In our world foreign languages are becoming more and more important.	
form teacher	*Klassenlehrer*	Mr Greeves is our new form teacher.	
grade [AE]	*(Schul-) Klasse, Jahrgangsstufe*	The Americans say 'grade' for 'class' or 'form'.	= form
grade [AE]	*Schulnote*	You need good grades to get a good job.	= mark
(to) hate	*hassen*	I always liked school, but my sister hated it.	
high school [AE]	*Oberstufenschule (14–18)*	After high school, Harry wants to go to university.	
(to) improve	*sich verbessern, besser machen/ werden*	One of the best ways for a girl to improve her English is to work as an au pair.	
(to) interrupt	*unterbrechen*	Noisy kids often interrupt the lessons.	
language course	*Sprachkurs*	An au pair should be given enough free time to go to language courses.	
(to) leave	*verlassen*	Steve left school and worked in a fast food restaurant.	= (to) finish school ≠ (to) start school

vocabulary	dt. Bedeutung	English sentence	syn/opp
lesson	*Unterrichtsstunde, Lektion*	Every Tuesday we have two English lessons.	
library	*Bücherei*	Jenny and Julie help organize our school library twice a week.	
mark	*Schulnote*	Oliver is working hard to get better marks in English and French.	= grade [AE]
maths	*Mathe (Kurzform)*	Hannah is not good at maths.	
oral	*mündlich*	I hate oral exams. I just get too nervous.	
(to) pass	*bestehen (eine Prüfung)*	Things are going well. I've just passed my exam.	
(to) prepare	*sich vorbereiten*	Pupils learn and prepare for exams.	= (to) get ready
pupil	*Schüler*	The number of pupils at private schools is rising.	= student
school fees	*Schulgeld, Schulgebühren*	At private schools pupils have to pay school fees of £ 10,000 a year or more.	
school holiday(s)	*Schulferien*	In my last school holidays I visited my aunt in Glasgow.	= vacation [AE]
school leaver	*Schulabgänger*	In Britain many young school leavers are out of work.	
school meal	*(Mittag-) Essen in der Schule*	Sally's favourite school meal is fish and chips.	= school lunch, school dinner
school trip	*Schulfahrt, Klassenreise*	Many parents say that school trips are too expensive.	= excursion
school uniform	*Schuluniform*	At British schools children wear school uniforms.	

vocabulary	dt. Bedeutung	English sentence	syn/opp
skill	*Fähigkeit, Fertigkeit*	At school young people learn lots of skills which will be useful for them in their jobs later on.	
(to) spell	*(richtig) schreiben, buchstabieren*	How do you spell this word, please?	
spelling	*Schreibung, Rechtschreibung*	Grandparents think that good spelling is more important than knowing about computers.	
subject	*Schulfach*	Most pupils think that English and maths are difficult subjects.	
(to) take an exam	*eine Prüfung machen*	British school children take their first exam when they are 7.	
talent	*Begabung*	Daniel has creative talent. He writes music.	= gift
test	*Klassenarbeit, Prüfung*	Debbie felt she had done well in her last maths test.	
trainee	*Praktikant, in der Ausbildung Stehender*	The wages for trainees are often very poor.	
training	*Ausbildung*	In England, many school leavers start a job without any training.	
vocabulary	*Wortschatz, Vokabular*	We have to take one vocabulary test every week.	
(to) worry	*sich sorgen*	Zoe worried about the result of her last English test.	
written test	*Klassenarbeit, schriftliche Arbeit*	I think I did very well in the last written test in English literature.	

Sports and Leisure Time

vocabulary	dt. Bedeutung	English sentence	syn/opp
(to) act	*handeln, sich benehmen, sich verhalten*	Don't act like a child, Dennis.	
action	*Handeln, Handlung, Aktion*	Most young people like films with a lot of action.	
active	*aktiv*	Sue is active in different groups where English and Indian children work together.	≠ inactive, lazy
activity	*(Freizeit-) Beschäftigung im Freien; Tätigkeit*	In the USA, sports are an important school activity.	≠ inactivity
adventure	*Abenteuer*	Captain James Cook's life was full of adventure.	
against	*gegen*	I taught myself to play chess, and I often played against the computer.	
amateur	*Amateur*	An amateur practises his sport without getting any money.	≠ profes-sional, pro
angry	*zornig*	My Dad was really angry when he saw the phone bill!	
athlete	*Athlet(in)*	The Aboriginal athlete Cathy Freeman is very popular in Australia.	
attack	*Angriff*	The trainer said, "Attack is the best form of defence."	≠ defence
audience	*Publikum, Zuschauer*	Rappers talk to their audience.	
backpack	*Rucksack*	Before starting on our tour I put enough food for three days in my backpack.	

vocabulary	dt. Bedeutung	English sentence	syn/opp
(to) bet	*wetten*	The British like betting on horses and dogs.	
boring	*langweilig*	Young people find TV documentaries boring.	
box office	*Kasse*	The box office will open at 6 o'clock.	
business	*Geschäft*	Robbie Williams went into show business when he was 15.	
canoeing	*Kanu fahren*	In the summer Julianne goes canoeing with her brother and father.	
(to) challenge	*herausfordern*	The young boxer will challenge the title holder.	
champion	*Sieger(in), Champion*	In 2005 Fernando Alonso became the youngest Formula 1 Champion in the world.	
(to) cheer cheerleader	*anfeuern* *Cheerleader (Mädchen, die die Zuschauer anfeuern)*	The fans cheer their team. Cheerleaders dress in the colours of their team.	
chess	*Schach*	When he was three Tom Hadfield taught himself to play chess.	
collect	*sammeln*	Do you collect music CDs or DVDs?	
collect stamps	*Briefmarken sammeln*	Collecting stamps is an interesting hobby.	
computer games	*Computerspiele*	Neil likes playing computer games and he often surfs the Internet, too.	

vocabulary	dt. Bedeutung	English sentence	syn/opp
cooking	*Kochen*	For some people cooking is a hobby, for others it's hard work.	
crowd	*Menge*	When England beat Germany in the 1966 football World Cup final the crowd went wild.	
cycling	*Radfahren*	The Tour de France is the world's most important cycling event.	
(to) decide	*entscheiden*	As it was raining we decided to go to the local museum.	
decision	*Entscheidung*	It was a good decision to stay out of the rain.	
(to) do aerobics	*Aerobic machen*	My neighbour does aerobics three times a week to keep fit.	
(to) do sport	*Sport treiben*	You should do more sport to keep fit.	
draw	*Unentschieden*	Our last three matches ended in a draw.	
entertainment	*Unterhaltung*	Sport has become part of the entertainment industry.	
equipment	*Ausrüstung*	Excellent sportsmen get their equipment free from sponsors.	
event	*Ereignis*	Tennis at Wimbledon is an important sporting event in the United Kingdom.	
exercise	*(körperliche) Bewegung, Training, Gymnastik*	The doctor told Sandra to do more exercise.	

vocabulary	dt. Bedeutung	English sentence	syn/opp
(to) exercise	*trainieren, üben*	You will become better, if you exercise every day.	
experience	*Erfahrung*	Our trip to Loch Ness in Scotland was a real experience.	
fair	*Markt, Jahrmarkt*	We spent the day looking through books at the book fair.	
fame	*Ruhm*	In Hollywood tourists walk along the Walk of Fame.	
famous	*berühmt*	On our trip to London we visited the famous wax show at Madame Tussauds.	
favourite	*Lieblings-*	Street basketball has become a favourite sport for kids.	
fight	*Kampf*	In boxing, many fights are decided on points.	
gardening	*Gartenarbeit*	My mother likes gardening, because she likes working in the fresh air.	
(to) get away	*entfliehen, entkommen*	At weekends we try to get away from the city – we go for walks in the country.	
(to) go (window) shopping	*Schaufensterbummel machen*	My aunts Mary and Mabel like to go window shopping. I hate it.	
(to) go for a walk	*einen Spaziergang machen*	After long hours of working in his office my father goes for a walk.	
ground	*Stadion*	FC Chelsea's home ground is called "Stamford Bridge".	= stadium

vocabulary	dt. Bedeutung	English sentence	syn/opp
gymnastics	*Turnen*	In gymnastics some world record holders are still at school.	
healthy health	*gesund* *Gesundheit*	Keep your body fit and healthy!	≠ unhealthy
hip	*Hüfte*	Hip jeans were very popular last summer.	
hooligan	*Rowdy*	Young football hooligans got into trouble with the police.	
indoors	*Hallen-*	On cold days we stayed indoors.	
inline-skating	*Inlineskates fahren*	Jack and Daniel are good friends. They taught themselves inline-skating.	
(to) be interested in	*Interesse haben an*	Most girls are interested in cosmetics and clothes.	
jogging	*Jogging*	Every morning at 6 my father goes jogging.	
(to) keep fit	*fit, gesund bleiben*	My neighbour does aerobics three times a week to keep fit.	
(to) last	*dauern*	A game of cricket lasts all day.	
latest	*neueste(r, s)*	Victoria always wears the latest fashion.	
leisure (time)	*Freizeit*	What interests do you have in your leisure time?	= free time, spare time
(to) listen to CDs / to the radio	*CDs/Radio hören*	Every Saturday afternoon I listen to the radio to get information about the day's football matches.	
live	*direkt (TV- oder Radiosendung)*	The football match will be shown live on TV.	≠ recorded

vocabulary	dt. Bedeutung	English sentence	syn/opp
(to) look forward to	*sich freuen auf*	James and his sister Laura are looking forward to their exchange year in America.	
manager	*Trainer*	Sir Alex Fergusson is one of the most successful football managers in Britain.	= trainer, coach
match	*Spiel*	"Match of the Day" is a popular programme on British television.	= game
(to) meet friends	*Freunde treffen*	I meet my friends in our local youth club every Friday night.	
member	*Mitglied*	James plays football and is a member of Manchester United FC.	
mountain biking	*Mountainbike fahren*	Last summer we went mountain biking in Scotland.	
musician	*Musiker*	Bruce Springsteen started his career as a musician in bars and clubs.	
Olympic Games	*Olympische Spiele*	At the Olympic Games in Athens 2004, athletes from the United Kingdom won nine gold medals.	
outdoor	*im Freien*	The holiday camp in Wales offers a lot of outdoor activities.	≠ indoor
pen friend	*Brieffreund*	My French pen friend Michelle will visit me next summer.	
(to) phone friends	*Freunde anrufen*	Phoning your friends on a mobile can be very expensive.	

vocabulary	dt. Bedeutung	English sentence	syn/opp
physical	*körperlich*	You have to do more physical exercise or you will get too fat!	
pitch	*Spielfeld*	A new cricket pitch was built for the training of the younger teams.	= field, sports ground
(to) play a musical instrument	*ein Musikinstrument spielen*	I was ten when I started playing an instrument.	
(to) play football	*Fußball spielen*	David Beckham started playing football when he was very young.	
(to) play in a band	*in einer Band spielen*	Have you ever played in a school band?	
(to) play on the computer	*am Computer spielen*	Bob's mother thinks that her son spends too much time playing on his computer.	
(to) play the guitar	*Gitarre spielen*	Andy Summers learnt to play the guitar when he was 14.	
(to) play the piano	*Klavier spielen*	Some kids start playing the piano when they are eight.	
popular	*beliebt*	Soccer is the most popular sport in England.	
(to) practise	*üben*	If you want to win, you have to practise a lot.	
(to) practise	*ausüben*	Most teenagers want to practise a sport or hobby.	
professional	*Profi-, Berufs-(sportler)*	A professional footballer can earn a lot of money in a short time.	≠ amateur

vocabulary	dt. Bedeutung	English sentence	syn/opp
record	*Rekord*	Franziska van Almsick set up her first swimming world record when she was 14.	
(to) relax	*sich entspannen*	During the long flight the passengers relaxed watching a film	
(to) ride a bike	*Fahrrad fahren*	Riding a bike is much healthier than going by car.	
rival	*Konkurrent*	Arsenal London and Chelsea are local rivals.	
rule	*Bestimmung, Verbot, Vorschrift*	Games are played to rules.	
(to) shout	*schreien*	The girls shouted, "Our team will win!"	
(to) sign a contract	*einen Vertrag unterschreiben*	At 18 basketballer LeBron James signed a contract with the Nike company.	
skateboarding	*Skateboard fahren*	West Hollywood kids enjoy skateboarding and listening to hip hop music.	
skiing	*Ski fahren*	We go skiing in Switzerland every year.	
soccer	*(europäischer) Fußball*	American football isn't the same as European football or soccer.	
sport event	*Sportveranstaltung*	People go to watch sport events because they find them exciting.	
sportsman	*Sportler*	Young Jonathan is a very good sportsman.	
stay	*Aufenthalt*	During our stay in New York we went for walks in Central Park.	

vocabulary	dt. Bedeutung	English sentence	syn/opp
(to) stay at a hotel	*in einem Hotel wohnen*	Staying at a hotel is more expensive than camping.	
stimulant	*Droge*	Sometimes sportsmen take stimulants to win.	= drug
success	*Erfolg*	The success of many athletes is hard work and fitness.	
successful	*erfolgreich*	Dirk Nowitzki is the most successful German basketball player.	
supporter	*(Fußball-) Anhänger*	I've always been a supporter of our local football team.	= fan
(to) surf the Internet	*im Internet surfen*	Surfing the internet for hours is cheaper today than in the past.	
(to) take a break	*eine Pause machen*	On our bike tour we took a break by the river.	
(to) take off	*starten*	You should arrive at the airport two hours before your plane takes off.	
(to) take part in	*teilnehmen an*	All students wanted to take part in the school trip to Cornwall.	
(to) take photos	*Fotos machen*	Sue takes photos for the school newspaper.	
(to) take place	*stattfinden*	Olympic games take place every four years.	
tourism	*Tourismus*	Tourism brings money to poor countries like Sri Lanka.	
tourist attraction	*Touristen-attraktion*	Disneyland in Florida offers many tourist attractions.	
track	*(Renn-) Bahn*	Young drivers can practise on special race tracks.	

vocabulary	dt. Bedeutung	English sentence	syn/opp
(to) train	*trainieren*	Top sportsmen have to train hard every day.	
trainer	*Trainer*	Our trainer does not like it when we are late for training.	
trainers	*Turnschuhe*	For my birthday my parents bought me cool orange-coloured trainers.	
travel agent	*Reisebüro-kaufmann, Reisebüro-kauffrau*	The travel agent worked out the prices for a caravan holiday in Ireland.	
travel agent's, travel agency	*Reisebüro*	I went to the travel agent's to pick up brochures.	
viewer	*Zuschauer*	MTV has more young viewers than any other TV station.	
violence	*Gewalttätigkeit*	Real football fans don't like violence.	
(to) visit places	*besichtigen*	On our trip to London we visited many interesting places.	
(to) vote	*wählen (zu); abstimmen*	Zinedine Zidane was voted "Player of the Year."	
(to) watch birds	*Vögel beobachten*	My sister has been watching birds for years. She knows all their names.	
(to) watch sport on TV	*Sport im Fernsehen sehen*	Luke shouldn't only watch sport on TV – he should go out and practise it.	
youth club	*Jugendclub*	Kevin and his friends meet at the local youth club to practise in the band.	
youth hostel	*Jugendherberge*	Our class stayed at a youth hostel in Devon.	

Teenage Life

vocabulary	dt. Bedeutung	English sentence	syn/opp
activity	*Tätigkeit, Aktivität; Unternehmung*	In the summer young people go hiking, canoeing or do other activities.	≠ inactivity
(to) admire	*bewundern*	I admire my grandfather. He started his business with almost no money at all when he was only 16.	≠ (to) look down on
admirer	*Verehrer/ Verehrerin*	My sister Jemma got a letter from a secret admirer.	
adult	*Erwachsene(r)*	In the USA you are an adult by law when you are old enough to vote.	≠ kid, youngster
advice	*Rat, Ratschlag, Ratschläge*	Marian didn't know what job offer to take, so she asked her dad for advice.	
(to) advise	*raten; beraten*	If you don't know what medicine to take, a doctor can advise you.	
against	*gegen*	Lots of young people revolt against their parents.	≠ for
(to) agree	*übereinstimmen, zustimmen*	Harry and his parents didn't agree about the boy's plans for the future.	≠ (to) disagree
agreement	*Zustimmung*	Bob and his friend Jeff made an agreement to help each other.	≠ disagree-ment
angry	*böse, wütend*	Dad was really angry when he saw the phone bill.	
(to) annoy	*jmdn. ärgern*	It really annoys me when people are late.	

vocabulary	dt. Bedeutung	English sentence	syn/opp
apart	*getrennt, entfernt*	My mother and father live apart.	
apartment [AE]	*Wohnung*	In our next holidays we're going to stay in an apartment for ten days.	= flat
(to) argue	*(sich) streiten*	I argue a lot with my parents about going out at weekends.	= (to) quarrel
(to) attack	*angreifen*	She attacked politicians for not doing enough for young people.	≠ (to) defend
attractive	*attraktiv, ansprechend*	Sheila likes Brad Pitt; she finds him very attractive.	
barbecue	*Grill; Grillfest*	I'm going to invite all my friends to a big barbecue to celebrate my birthday.	
beautiful **beauty**	*schön* *Schönheit*	Josie has a beautiful smile. Jessica wanted to take part in a beauty competition, but her parents were against it.	≠ ugly
(to) behave	*sich benehmen*	I hope you behave yourself while your mother is away.	
behaviour	*Verhalten, Benehmen*	During my aunt's visit I put on my best behaviour.	
(to) blame	*die Schuld geben*	Why do people always blame others for their own mistakes?	
boastful	*angeberisch, prahlerisch*	Some Canadians think all Americans are noisy and boastful.	≠ shy
brilliant	*toll, glänzend, großartig*	The time I spent with my friend Michelle in France was brilliant.	

vocabulary	dt. Bedeutung	English sentence	syn/opp
broke	*pleite*	I cannot buy a new bike. I'm broke.	≠ rich
(to) care	*sich kümmern (um etwas), (etwas) wichtig nehmen*	Most young people care about the environment.	
careful	*vorsichtig, sorgfältig*	When you walk around in New York be careful. Don't talk to strangers.	≠ careless
casual	*leger, lässig*	I like wearing casual clothes.	≠ formal
(to) chat	*sich unterhalten, plaudern*	Kevin likes to chat with his friends on the internet.	= talk
clothes	*Kleidung, Kleider*	My grandmother made all the clothes for her children.	
confident	*selbstsicher*	Sarah seems very confident about her exam.	≠ shy, embarrassed
curfew	*Ausgangssperre für Teenager*	In some big cities in America teenagers cannot be "outside the home" at night because of the teen curfew.	
cute	*süß, niedlich*	I've met a boy, Grandma. He's real cute.	
date	*Verabredung*	Do you think I can ask Naomi to go on a date with me?	
dedication	*Widmung*	Out teacher was impressed by the dedication with which we worked for the school magazine.	≠ disinterest

vocabulary	dt. Bedeutung	English sentence	syn/opp
depressed	*deprimiert, niedergeschlagen*	Laura felt depressed when she looked at the thin models in the magazines, because she thought she was not as slim as them.	≠ pleased, satisfied
diary	*Tagebuch*	Since she was ten Sandra has kept a diary.	
(to) disagree	*anderer Meinung sein; nicht übereinstimmen*	My dad and I disagree about most things.	≠ (to) agree
(to) discriminate	*diskriminieren, benachteiligen*	It is not right to discriminate against people because of their colour or religion.	≠ (to) accept, (to) tolerate
discrimination	*Diskriminierung, Benachteiligung*	There is still discrimination against black people.	≠ tolerance, integration
(to) discuss	*diskutieren, besprechen*	I discussed my plans to work during the summer holidays with my parents.	= (to) talk about
duty	*Pflicht*	As a pupil it is your duty to go to school regularly.	
embarrassed	*verlegen*	I get very embarrassed when my mom gives me a kiss in front of my friends.	= shy ≠ confident
(to) encourage	*ermutigen, ermuntern*	My sports teacher encouraged me to take part in local competitions.	≠ (to) discourage
(to) enjoy	*sich freuen, genießen*	Youth centres are important places where young people can enjoy themselves.	
enthusiastic	*enthusiastisch, begeistert; begeisterungsfähig*	My parents were enthusiastic about my idea of spending a school year in the USA.	≠ bored

vocabulary	dt. Bedeutung	English sentence	syn/opp
exhausted	*erschöpft*	After cross country running Michael was so exhausted that he went to bed straight away.	≠ fit
fact	*Tatsache*	Nancy tried to hide the fact that she was nervous by speaking quickly.	
(to) fall in love	*sich verlieben*	Sue was fourteen when she fell in love for the first time.	
fame	*Ruhm*	Orlando Bloom found fame as an actor.	
famous	*berühmt*	Many famous actors live in Beverly Hills.	≠ unknown
(to) fancy	*eine Schwäche für jmdn. haben*	My sister is mad on Johnny Depp – she rather fancies him.	
fault	*Schuld, Fehler*	Perhaps it is your own fault if you can't find any friends.	= mistake
fed up	*die Nase voll haben*	My mother was fed up with me because my room was in such a mess.	
friendly	*freundlich*	In the summer camp we met a lot of friendly people from all over the world.	= kind ≠ unfriendly, unkind
(to) frighten	*erschrecken*	When the teacher shouted at me I was terribly frightened.	
glad	*froh*	I was glad that I had taken part in the exchange visit.	≠ sad
gossip	*Klatsch, Tratsch*	I heard some gossip about Phil and Janette, but I don't believe it.	
(to) grow up	*erwachsen werden*	Girls grow up more quickly than boys.	

vocabulary	dt. Bedeutung	English sentence	syn/opp
guidance	*Beratung, (An-) Leitung, Führung*	Some youngsters won't accept guidance from their parents.	
happy	*glücklich*	Tom is happy because Sarah loves him too.	≠ unhappy
health	*Gesundheit*	I told my older sister that smoking was bad for her health.	
helpful	*hilfreich*	Teachers at my school are friendly and helpful.	
hero	*Held(in)*	Do you have an everyday hero?	
highlight	*Höhepunkt*	The helicopter flight over the Grand Canyon was the highlight of our US tour.	
(to) hike	*wandern*	It's difficult to hike down to the bottom of the canyon and back on the same day.	
homeless	*heimatlos, obdachlos*	At my school we collect clothes for homeless people once a year.	
independence	*Unabhängigkeit*	When Simon earned his first money he had a feeling of independence.	≠ dependency
independent	*unabhängig*	Most young people want to become independent from their parents.	≠ dependent
influence **(to) influence**	*Einfluss* *beeinflussen*	My dad says that I am under the influence of my friends too much.	
instead	*stattdessen*	We told Nick to work harder instead of fooling around.	
interest	*Interesse*	My parents take an interest in my work at school.	≠ disinterest

vocabulary	dt. Bedeutung	English sentence	syn/opp
(to) introduce	*einführen; vorstellen*	The government introduced a new programme for school leavers.	
kick	*Nervenkitzel, Kick, berauschende Wirkung*	Lynn gets her kicks by bungee jumping.	
kind	*freundlich*	It pays to be kind to other people.	= friendly ≠ unkind, unfriendly
latest	*neueste(-r,-s)*	In my free time after school I enjoy watching the latest videos with my friends.	
lifestyle	*Lebensstil*	Many young people are looking for an alternative lifestyle.	
lively	*lebhaft*	We had a very lively discussion about how much pocket-money a week kids should get.	
(to) lose	*verlieren*	I would like to work abroad, but I don't want to lose my friends.	≠ (to) win
loyal	*treu*	Miriam has always been very loyal to her friends.	
(to) mean	*bedeuten; meinen*	Real friendship means a lot to me.	
messy	*unordentlich; schmutzig*	My mother hates it when my bedroom is so messy.	≠ tidy, clean
(to) miss	*vermissen*	When Anne worked as an au-pair in America she missed her family and friends and felt a bit lonely.	
(to) miss	*versäumen, verpassen*	This year I haven't missed a single day at school.	

vocabulary	dt. Bedeutung	English sentence	syn/opp
nervous	*nervös*	Raymond was rather nervous when he went for his first job interview.	≠ confident
old-fashioned	*altmodisch*	My grandparents have rather old-fashioned ideas about young people.	≠ modern, up-to-date
opinion	*Meinung*	In my opinion we should do more for our environment.	= view
opposite	*Gegenteil*	Ursula often does the opposite of what her mother tells her to do.	
ordinary	*gewöhnlich, normal*	In Germany we don't have school uniforms. You come to school in your ordinary clothes.	= normal, usual ≠ extra-ordinary, unusual
(to) owe	*jmdm. etwas schulden*	Marc knows that he owes his success to his parents.	
pleased	*zufrieden; erfreut*	As Mike had done well in his exam he felt pleased with himself.	≠ disap-pointed, depressed, sad
pocket-money	*Taschengeld*	Do you think you get enough pocket-money?	
proud	*stolz*	Hannah was proud when she won the scholarship to Oxford University.	
quiet	*still, ruhig*	When the director of the school came into our classroom everybody went quiet.	≠ loud, noisy
relationship (with)	*Beziehung (zu), Verhältnis (zu)*	Helen's relationship with her parents has become better since she moved to another town.	

vocabulary	dt. Bedeutung	English sentence	syn/opp
(to) relax	*sich entspannen*	My father finds it very difficult to relax – he works all the time.	= (to) rest
(to) respect	*respektieren*	I don't agree with what you said, but I respect your opinion.	
role	*Rolle*	My grandmother played an important role in my childhood.	
secret	*Geheimnis*	My little sister can't keep a secret.	
serious	*ernst, ernsthaft; seriös*	I told my parents that I was serious about spending a year at an American college.	
(to) shout	*schreien, rufen*	Nobody likes to be shouted at.	≠ (to) whisper
shy	*scheu, schüchtern*	Don't be shy! Ask for help when you need it.	≠ confident
slim	*schlank*	It's not right when young girls want to be as slim as fashion models.	≠ fat
society	*Gesellschaft*	Some young people think it is hard to find a place in society.	
stamina	*Ausdauer; Durchhalte-vermögen*	If you want to train for a marathon you need a lot of stamina.	
strange	*seltsam, eigenartig*	Wearing a uniform was a strange experience for Chris when he went to an English school for the first time.	≠ familiar
suggestion	*Vorschlag*	Stuart's parents didn't like his suggestion of leaving school as soon as possible.	

vocabulary	dt. Bedeutung	English sentence	syn/opp
(to) support	*unterstützen, fördern*	My parents have always supported me, I'm glad to say.	
survey	*Umfrage*	Another survey was made to find out what sort of music teenagers really like.	
(to) tolerate	*dulden; sich gefallen lassen*	Our form teacher does not tolerate bad behaviour in class.	
topic	*Thema*	Only very few teenagers are interested in political topics.	= subject
tough	*hart*	Starting work is sometimes very tough.	= hard ≠ easy; soft, weak
trouble	*Schwierigkeiten, Ärger*	More young people will get into trouble with the police when they take drugs.	
uncomfortable	*ungemütlich, unbequem*	I lied to my parents; that's why I felt very uncomfortable.	= uneasy ≠ comfortable
unhappy	*unglücklich*	Sharon was unhappy because she didn't hear from Alec for three weeks.	≠ happy, glad, pleased
worried	*beunruhigt*	Megan was worried about the big exam at the end of the semester.	= troubled
worse	*schlechter, schlimmer*	My English isn't very good and my French is even worse.	≠ better

Work

vocabulary	dt. Bedeutung	English sentence	syn/opp
(to) be able	*etw. tun können, fähig sein*	Mohammed hasn't been able to find a job yet because he doesn't speak English very well.	≠ unable
ability	*Können, Fähigkeit*	It is not always easy to find a job which suits one's abilities.	= capability, talent ≠ inability, disability
abroad	*im Ausland*	Lisa is interested in working abroad, especially in Ireland or the USA.	
(to) advertise	*inserieren, werben*	If a firm wants to sell more of a product, it has to advertise.	
advert, advertisement	*Anzeige, Annonce*	Ron saw an advert in the Sheffield News for a job as an assistant this summer.	
advice	*Rat*	Before you choose a job, get some expert advice.	
(to) advise	*raten*	If you don't know what sort of job you would like to do an expert can advise you.	
application	*Bewerbung*	I sent my application for a job to Barclays Bank yesterday.	
application form	*Bewerbungs-formular*	When I started my new job I had to fill in lots of application forms.	
(to) apply for a job	*sich um eine Stelle bewerben*	After leaving school, Harry applied for a job with several firms.	
apprentice	*Lehrling, Auszubildender*	Our baker needs a new apprentice.	

vocabulary	dt. Bedeutung	English sentence	syn/opp
apprenticeship	*Lehrzeit, Lehre*	During his apprenticeship Ed didn't earn a lot of money.	
assembly line	*Fließband*	On an assembly line, the parts of a car are put together.	
(to) be out of work	*arbeitslos sein*	Being out of work makes people feel depressed.	
(to) become	*werden*	Marvin said he didn't want to work in an office. He wanted to become an actor.	
(to) boom	*blühen, einen Aufschwung erleben*	The computer industry is really booming.	
boss	*Chef*	Marc always has to work late when the boss is away.	
business	*Geschäft, Betrieb*	When I've finished school, I'll work in my parents' business.	
busy	*hektisch, belebt, beschäftigt*	My first weeks at work have been very busy: I've been working hard from morning to evening.	
by trade	*von Beruf*	Oliver is a mechanic by trade.	
call centre	*telefonischer Kundendienst*	People who work in a call centre are on the phone all day.	
careers officer	*Berufsberater*	A careers officer informed us about jobs at the airport.	
challenge	*Herausforderung*	Some people look for a special challenge and work abroad.	

vocabulary	dt. Bedeutung	English sentence	syn/opp
child labour	*Kinderarbeit*	Child labour is a big problem in poor countries: young children work in factories.	
choice	*Wahl*	What would you like to do? The choice is yours.	
(to) choose	*wählen, aussuchen*	At Lloyds Bank they choose from the best candidates.	
company	*Firma*	The new video game will earn a lot of money for our company.	= business, firm
customer	*Kunde*	The firm won new customers abroad.	= client
CV (curriculum vitae)	*Lebenslauf*	CV is short for the Latin "curriculum vitae".	
(to) develop	*entwickeln*	Kai Krause develops new software in Silicon Valley, California.	
dole (money)	*Arbeitslosengeld, Arbeitslosenunterstützung*	As he was out of work Steven received dole money.	
(to) earn	*verdienen*	In the USA blacks still earn less than whites.	
(to) earn one's living	*seinen Lebensunterhalt verdienen*	How do you earn your living?	
electrician	*Elektriker*	When all the lights went out in her house Mrs Cooper needed an electrician.	
(to) employ	*beschäftigen, anstellen*	The two largest firms in our town employ more than a thousand people each.	= (to) hire ≠ (to) fire

vocabulary	dt. Bedeutung	English sentence	syn/opp
employer	*Arbeitgeber*	The government is one of the largest employers in our country.	
employment	*Beschäftigung, Arbeit*	Meryl Taylor is looking for employment as a waitress.	
engine	*Motor*	Early in the 18th century the steam engine was invented.	= motor
engineer	*Ingenieur, Techniker*	Geoff is interested in technology. He wants to become an engineer when he leaves school.	
equipment	*Ausstattung, Einrichtung*	In his office Dean Harris has all the latest equipment like computers, copiers etc.	
experience	*Erfahrung*	Most pupils in Britain do work experience when they are 14 or 15.	
expert	*Fachmann*	Brian knows everything about computers. He has become a real expert.	
factory	*Fabrik*	More people work in banks and offices than in factories.	= works
(to) fill a position	*eine Stelle besetzen*	IBM is looking for a first-class applicant to fill the position of sales manager.	
firm	*Firma*	Alwyn lost his job as a driver when his firm closed.	= company
flexitime	*Gleitzeit*	Some companies have flexitime, which means that people can decide when their workday starts and finishes.	

vocabulary	dt. Bedeutung	English sentence	syn/opp
full-time	*Vollzeit, ganztägig, Ganztags-*	Mary and Sean have just got married and they both work full-time.	
full-time job	*Vollzeit-, Ganztagsarbeit*	Linda Hindes gave up her full-time job with the NatWest Bank to spend more time with her baby daughter Laura.	
(to) get a rise	*eine Lohnerhöhung bekommen*	Brian Kelly has just got a rise of 50 pounds a month.	
(to) hire	*einstellen*	American firms hire quickly – and fire quickly as well.	
(to) hire	*mieten*	My boss always hires cars from the same firm: Avis.	
income	*Einkommen, Einkünfte*	Many people who work in the City of London have a high income.	
(to) increase	*zunehmen*	The number of German firms which produce abroad may increase in the future.	
industry	*Industrie (-zweig), Gewerbe*	The shipbuilding industry is in great trouble today.	
industrial	*industriell*	The Industrial Revolution began in England in the eighteenth century.	
interview	*Vorstellung (-sgespräch)*	Sharon went for an interview with a manager of the Royal Bank of Scotland.	
job	*Beruf, Beschäftigung, Stellung*	Rita has found an exciting job as tourist guide in York.	

vocabulary	dt. Bedeutung	English sentence	syn/opp
job centre	*Arbeitsamt*	The job centre offers summer jobs for young people.	= labor office [AE], labour exchange
job interview	*Vorstellungs-gespräch*	Before you go to a job interview try to get as much information as possible about the firm in question.	
job market	*Arbeitsmarkt*	What effect will internet sales have on the job market?	= labour market, employment market
(to) have a regular job	*eine feste Stelle haben*	Gregory has a regular job as a mechanic.	
knowledge	*Kenntnisse, Wissen*	A good knowledge of Science and Maths is more important than good grades in Music and Art.	
labour	*Arbeit, Arbeitskräfte*	Many firms produce in India and Bangladesh because labour is cheap there.	
labour exchange	*Arbeitsamt*	Every morning Gary goes to the labour exchange to find out about new jobs.	= job centre, labour office
(to) live on	*leben von*	Denny, who works in a fast-food restaurant, has to live on very little money.	
machine	*Maschine*	Lazy people draw money from a machine through the window of their automobile.	
market	*Markt*	Sue Miller opened a shop at Camden Lock, London's most popular market.	

vocabulary	dt. Bedeutung	English sentence	syn/opp
motivated	*motiviert*	Tina was very motivated when she started her new job.	
(to) offer	*anbieten*	Most schools offer special training courses for school leavers.	
offer	*Angebot*	Liam accepted the new job offer.	
office	*Büro*	Jemma works in the BBC office in Birmingham.	
(to) order	*bestellen*	Lots of people order their books on the Internet.	
order	*Bestellung, Auftrag*	We thank you for your order of 25 Macintosh computers.	
(to) organise	*organisieren, planen*	Ken organises trips to the Florida Everglades.	
part-time	*Teilzeit-, Halbtags-*	Natalie has a part-time job because she has to look after her baby son.	
pay, payment	*Bezahlung, Lohn*	Vince Vaughn works as a security guard but his pay is rather low.	= wage, salary
position	*Stellung*	Iain Morris took up his position as Assistant Manager in January.	= post, job
(to) practise	*üben*	Michael practises his Spanish because he wants to work in South America.	
(to) prepare	*vorbereiten*	Debora prepared some answers for her job interview in London.	
preparation	*Vorbereitung*	My preparation for the job interview is almost complete.	

vocabulary	dt. Bedeutung	English sentence	syn/opp
(to) produce	*herstellen, erzeugen*	General Motors produces thousands of cars every year.	= (to) make
product	*Produkt, Erzeugnis*	"Our latest software product sells really well", the boss said.	
production	*Produktion, Herstellung*	Steven Spielberg started the production of his new film in Austria.	
profession	*Beruf (meistens mit Studium)*	For a profession (for example dentist or teacher) you have to study at a university.	
professional	*Profi-, Berufs-*	In the USA, professional basketball players earn millions of dollars.	≠ amateur
qualification	*Eignung; Vorbildung*	If you do not have good qualifications, it is very hard to find a job.	
(to) raise	*aufziehen*	Oliver got a full-time job and started to raise a family.	
(to) retire	*in Pension gehen, in Rente gehen, sich pensionieren lassen*	Workers retire at the age of 65.	≠ (to) start work
(to) run a firm	*eine Firma leiten*	Jim Goodwin is running the firm which his father started 45 years ago.	
salary	*Gehalt (Geld)*	Donna Birch's salary has gone up to £ 24,900 a year.	= wage, pay
self-employed	*selbstständig*	People who are self-employed usually work alone and have to do everything themselves.	

vocabulary	dt. Bedeutung	English sentence	syn/opp
shift	*Schicht, Arbeitsschicht*	All his life William Peel has been working night shift.	
skill	*Fertigkeit, Kenntnisse, Qualifikation*	I went on a training course because I wanted to improve my skills.	
skilled worker	*Facharbeiter*	A skilled worker has greater chances of finding a good job.	≠ unskilled worker
staff	*Belegschaft*	The director was pleased about the good work of the whole staff.	= workforce
stress	*Belastung, Stress, Spannung, Druck*	Before tests many pupils feel under stress.	
stressful	*anstrengend, aufreibend, stressig*	Many businessmen have a stressful job these days.	
(to) take days off	*frei nehmen*	Stewart felt ill, so he took a few days off work.	
technology	*Technik, Technology*	Young people are interested in the latest communication technology.	
tool	*Werkzeug, Gerät*	If you want to repair a car, you need the right tools.	
tough	*hart*	Driving a lorry is a tough job.	= hard ≠ easy
trade	*Handel, Handelsverkehr*	Trade between Europe and China has increased.	= business
trade union	*Gewerkschaft*	In the nineteenth century the first trade union was formed in England.	= labor union [AE]
(to) train	*ausbilden, abrichten, dressieren*	Bill has always liked dogs. He now trains the dogs of other people.	

vocabulary	dt. Bedeutung	English sentence	syn/opp
trainee	*Praktikant, Lehrling*	Richard works as a trainee reporter for "Home News".	
training	*Ausbildung*	When Pamela Hall started in her new job, she was first given computer training.	
training course	*Ausbildungskurs*	There are special training courses for school leavers who do not have a job.	
unemployed	*arbeitslos*	Unemployed school leavers get help from the government.	= jobless, out of work
unemployment	*Arbeitslosigkeit*	Unemployment is one of the greatest problems today.	
unskilled	*ungelernt, nicht ausgebildet*	Unskilled workers can lose their jobs quickly.	≠ skilled
wage	*Lohn, Arbeitslohn*	As a carpenter he gets a wage of 420 pounds a week.	= pay
work	*Arbeit*	What sort of work would you like best?	
(to) work overtime	*Überstunden machen*	Mr Taylor likes working overtime, because with the extra money he can take his family on holiday.	
(to) work shifts	*Schicht arbeiten*	In the newspaper printing plant, we work 24 hour shifts.	
working condition	*Arbeitsbedingung*	The trade unions fight for better working conditions.	
working hours	*Arbeitszeit, Arbeitsstunden*	People working in factories would like shorter working hours.	
workshop	*Arbeitsgemeinschaft; Werkstatt*	Are you interested in a workshop on computer programming?	

Media

vocabulary	dt. Bedeutung	English sentence	syn/opp
address	*Adresse*	In a letter you write your address first, then the date.	
answer phone [BE]	*Anrufbeantworter*	You can leave a message on an answering machine.	= answering machine [AE]
audience	*Publikum, Zuschauer*	Rappers talk to their audience.	
bookshelf	*Bücherregal, Bücherregale*	So many books! Mavis bought a new bookshelf.	
boring	*langweilig*	Most papers contain a lot of boring information.	
(to) borrow	*(sich) borgen, (sich) ausleihen*	Could I borrow the latest CD which you bought?	
brochure	*Broschüre*	I sent for a brochure about national parks in the USA.	
button	*Knopf*	"You push this button here to start the programme."	= key
at the push of a button	*auf Knopfdruck*	You can surf the Internet at the push of a button.	
(to) call	*anrufen*	I'll call you tomorrow.	
CD	*CD (Compact Disk)*	a disk which contains music or computer data	
cell phone [AE]	*Handy, Mobiltelefon*	All young people like cell phones.	= mobile phone [BE]
channel	*Fernsehkanal, -sender*	MTV is a popular TV channel.	
(to) choose	*auswählen*	On MTV kids choose the coolest singer by voting online.	
choice	*Wahl*	Today you have a wide choice of computer games.	

vocabulary	dt. Bedeutung	English sentence	syn/opp
(to) click (on) a button	*auf eine Schaltfläche klicken*	Click this button to end the programme.	
communication	*Kommunikation*	Communication with family and friends has become much easier today.	
computer application	*Computeranwendung, Informatik*	Paul did a computer application course at his school.	
computer scientist	*Informatiker*	Computer scientists are working on the "thinking computer".	
(to) connect	*verbinden*	All of the PCs in our school are connected to a central computer.	
connection	*Verbindung*	If you have a fast internet connection, you can download pictures quickly.	
(to) create	*schaffen, erschaffen*	The World Wide Web was created in the early 1990s.	
(to) deliver	*austragen, zustellen; liefern*	A lot of young people deliver newspapers to earn some extra money.	
(to) design	*entwerfen, gestalten*	Helen knows how to design a webpage.	
desk	*Schreibtisch*	I have a new desk on which I can do my homework.	
diary	*Tagebuch*	Sandra has kept a diary since she was 10.	
dictionary	*Wörterbuch*	You can look up new words in a dictionary on the internet.	

vocabulary	dt. Bedeutung	English sentence	syn/opp
(to) draw	*zeichnen*	Our teacher asked me to draw a few pictures for the school magazine.	
drive (in a computer)	*Laufwerk*	Today, all computers have a CD-ROM drive.	
e-mail (= electronic mail)	*E-Mail (= elektronische Post)*	Every day I send e-mails to my friends.	
(to) enter	*eingeben (Benutzernamen und Passwort)*	Please enter your name and password here.	
(to) enter	*eintreten*	Be careful when you enter the old library.	
envelope	*Briefumschlag*	Dave put the letter in its envelope and took it to the postbox.	
expert	*Fachmann*	Some of my friends are real computer experts.	= specialist
felt-tip	*Filzstift*		
folder	*Verzeichnis; Ordner; Aktenordner*	I cannot remember in which folder I saved my essay.	= directory
(to) function	*funktionieren*	My new laptop computer functions perfectly.	
(to) guide	*führen, leiten*	A new technique was invented to guide and control a rocket.	
hard disk	*Festplatte*	My music files take up a lot of room on my hard disk.	= hard drive
homepage	*Ausgangsseite (im Internet)*		
(to) infect	*infizieren, anstecken*	A computer virus infected computers around the world.	

vocabulary	dt. Bedeutung	English sentence	syn/opp
information	*Information(en), Auskunft*	On the internet you can find some information about almost any topic.	
ink	*Tinte*		
(to) install	*aufstellen, installieren*	Mr Reeves installed a new computer in his office.	
(to) interview	*interviewen, befragen*	The reporter interviewed David Beckham after the match.	
(to) introduce	*einführen*	Many firms introduce computers in order to make production cheaper.	
isolated (to) isolate isolation	*einsam* *isolieren* *Isolation, Absonderung*	Do computer users become more isolated?	= lonely
(to) keep in touch	*in Verbindung bleiben*	It is easy to keep in touch by sending e-mails.	≠ (to) lose touch
key	*Taste; Schlüssel*	Press any key to continue.	= button
keyboard	*Tastatur*	Mary-Ann's fingers moved quickly around the keyboard.	
language	*Sprache*	English is the world's most important language.	
letter	*Brief*	I got a letter from my friend Desmond yesterday.	
letter	*Buchstabe*	"A" is the first letter of the alphabet.	
library	*Bücherei*	In the afternoon we often go to the library to borrow new books.	
literature	*Literatur*	Ireland is famous for its countryside, its literature and its music.	

vocabulary	dt. Bedeutung	English sentence	syn/opp
live [ai]	*direkt*	Many things can go wrong in a live TV show.	
magazine	*Zeitschrift*	The Big Issue is a magazine which is written by people who haven't got a home.	
mail	*Post*	The invitation arrived by mail this morning.	
mailbox	*Mailbox (eine Art Computerbrief-kasten)*	There are often too many unimportant messages in my mailbox.	
mailman [AE]	*Briefträger, Postbote*	Melinda's dad is a mailman in New York.	= postman [BE]
means means of com-munication means of transport	*Mittel* *Kommunikations-mittel* *Verkehrsmittel*	Young people like using the latest means of communication.	
media	*Medien*	Media are, for example: television, radio, news-papers and the internet	
message	*Nachricht, Botschaft*	I left a message for my parents telling them I would be back by 10 o'clock.	
mobile (phone)	*Handy, Mobiltelefon*	Text messages can be sent by computer or mobile phone.	= cellular phone, cell phone
news	*Nachrichten*	Have you heard the news today?	
newspaper	*Zeitung*	Sue read an article about the Sioux Indians in our local newspaper.	
(to) notice	*bemerken*	I noticed that I had forgotten to put a stamp on the envelope.	

vocabulary	dt. Bedeutung	English sentence	syn/opp
notice-board	*Anschlagbrett, schwarzes Brett*	The exam results will be put up on the notice-board.	
on the Internet	*im Internet*	It is easy to find information on the Internet.	= on the web
parcel	*Paket*	On my birthday the postman brought me a parcel from my auntie Jean in Wales.	
pen	*Füller*	I got pen and paper and wrote to my grandparents.	
pencil	*Bleistift*	Mr Norman always has a pencil behind his right ear.	
pen-friend [BE]	*Brieffreund(in)*	Hilary has pen-friends in India and Australia.	= pen-pal [AE]
photocopy	*fotokopieren*	I photocopied two articles from our school magazine.	
postcard	*Postkarte, Ansichtskarte*	My uncle Ted is on a world trip. He sends me postcards from the big cities he visits.	
post office	*Postamt*	I must take this parcel to the post office before six.	
postman	*Briefträger, Postbote*	Our postman usually comes before ten in the morning.	
programme	*Sendung*	What is your favourite TV programme?	
publicity	*Werbung; Publicity*	Good publicity is important if you want to sell your product.	
(to) receive **receiver** **reception**	*empfangen* *Empfänger; Telefonhörer* *Empfang*	With some mobile phones you can send and receive pictures.	

vocabulary	dt. Bedeutung	English sentence	syn/opp
(to) record	*aufzeichnen, aufnehmen*	I sometimes record a television programme when it starts after 10 at night.	
report	*Bericht*	Malcolm wrote a report about his school project.	
(to) ring	*anrufen; klingeln*	I rang Melanie to tell her about the film I had just seen.	
ring tone	*Klingelton*	Young people spend a lot of money on ring tones.	
satellite	*Satellit*	Sputnik 1 was the first Russian satellite in space.	
(to) save	*sichern, speichern (eine Datei)*	Save all your English documents in the same folder.	
search engine (to) search	*Suchmaschine* *suchen*	Google is the most the successful internet search engine.	
(to) send	*senden, schicken*	Don't forget to send me a postcard when you are in New Zealand!	
sincerely	*Mit freund-lichen/herzlichen Grüßen*	Yours sincerely, …	
SMS	*(Abk.: Short Message Service) Kurznachricht*	Young people use SMS more often than e-mail.	
stamp	*Briefmarke*	I posted a letter but forgot to put a stamp on it: That's why it came back the following day.	

vocabulary	dt. Bedeutung	English sentence	syn/opp
(to) store	*speichern*	You can store more text and pictures on a DVD than on a CD.	= (to) save
technical technique	*technisch, fachlich, Fach-*	These technical problems can only be solved by experts.	
technology	*Technologie*	In England, 14-year-olds have to take a test in information and communications technology.	
television	*Fernsehen*	Television has become the most powerful of all media today.	
texting	*Schreiben von SMS*	Young people prefer texting to writing letters.	
(to) text	*eine SMS schreiben*		
text message	*SMS*	Writing text messages is cheaper than calling.	
(to) turn off (the computer)	*den Computer ausschalten*	For some kids it is very hard to turn off the computer.	= (to) switch off ≠ (to) switch on, (to) turn on
virtual	*virtuell; nicht echt, nicht in Wirklichkeit vorhanden, nur im Internet*	An English website offers a virtual tour of Stonehenge.	
virus	*Virus*	Many computer viruses were written by teenagers.	= worm

Environment

vocabulary	dt. Bedeutung	English sentence	syn/opp
air pollution	*Luftverschmutzung*	Air pollution is a big problem today.	
alternative	*Alternative, andere Möglichkeit*	Wind energy is an alternative to nuclear energy.	
animal	*Tier*	The WWF works hard to save the lives of wild animals such as the Siberian tiger.	
atmosphere	*Atmosphäre*	The atmosphere protects the Earth.	
atomic energy	*Atomenergie*	Is atomic energy the answer to our energy problems?	= nuclear energy
average	*Durchschnitts-, durchschnittlich*	The summer was warm – with an average temperature of 23°C.	
bay	*Bucht*	A big earthquake hit the San Francisco Bay area in October 1989, and 62 people died.	
(to) burn	*(ver-, nieder-) brennen*	In South America farmers burn down huge forests.	
catastrophe	*Katastrophe*	Hurricane Katrina was a catastrophe which destroyed many houses.	= disaster
chemical	*Chemikalie*	We use too many chemicals in the house.	
(to) clean	*säubern, reinigen, aufräumen*	Every year in spring our youth group cleans up part of the river Avon.	

vocabulary	dt. Bedeutung	English sentence	syn/opp
cliff	*Klippe, Felsen*	From the cliffs of Dover you have a fantastic view across the English Channel.	
climate	*Klima*	Experts tell us that the climate of the earth will change.	
climate change	*Klimaänderung*	The climate change favours the mosquito that carries the malaria disease.	
cloud	*Wolke*	A fire in a Russian nuclear power station sent a radioactive cloud across Europe.	
coal	*Kohle*	On many Indian reservations coal and oil were found.	
coast	*Küste*	On the coast the climate is mild.	
countryside	*Landschaft, Gegend*	Keep our countryside clean and beautiful.	
danger	*Gefahr*	There is the danger that rare animals and plants will die out.	
dangerous	*gefährlich*	Lying in the sun too long can be dangerous to the skin.	≠ safe
degree	*Grad*	In the Arctic the temperature can drop to minus 50 degrees Celsius.	
desert	*Wüste*	In the desert it can be as hot as 54 degrees Celsius in the summer.	
(to) destroy	*zerstören*	We must not destroy more of our environment.	≠ (to) save

vocabulary	dt. Bedeutung	English sentence	syn/opp
destruction	*Zerstörung*	Let us stop the destruction of our forests!	
developed countries	*Industriestaaten, Industrieländer*	The developed countries should help the poorer ones.	= industrialized countries ≠ developing countries, Third World countries
(to) die out	*aussterben*	Many wild animals are about to die out.	≠ (to) survive
dirt	*Schmutz, Dreck*	I cannot stand the dirt and terrible noise of big cities.	
disaster	*Unglück*	The oil tanker accident was a disaster for the Spanish and French coasts.	= catastrophe
(to) dry up	*austrocknen, vertrocknen*	When it doesn't rain for a long time many rivers dry up.	
dump	*Müllhalde*	We must not use the oceans as cheap dumps.	
(to) dump	*abladen, ablagern*	Old car tyres have been dumped into the woods.	
earth	*Erde*	Death Valley is the hottest place on earth.	
earthquake	*Erdbeben*	In 1906 an earthquake in San Francisco killed 700 people.	
effect	*Wirkung, Auswirkung*	What will be the effects of changing temperatures on plants and animals?	
electricity	*Elektrizität*	Even today the Amish people in America don't use cars or electricity.	= (electric) power

vocabulary	dt. Bedeutung	English sentence	syn/opp
energy	*Energie*	In our homes we should try to save energy.	
environment	*Umwelt*	The environment is the natural world around us in which people, animals and plants live.	
environmental	*Umwelt-*	Young people are interested in environmental organisations such as the World Wildlife Fund (WWF) or Greenpeace.	
fog	*Nebel*	In the autumn we get a lot of fog, rain, and wind.	
forecast	*Vorhersage*	It is best to listen to the weather forecast before you go into the mountains.	
forest	*(größerer) Wald*	The rain forest in the Amazon is important for the climate on earth.	
fossil fuel	*fossiler Brennstoff*	Coal and natural gas are examples of fossil fuel.	
freeze	*(er-) frieren, gefrieren, erstarren*	If the sun shines less we will freeze.	≠ (to) melt
freezing	*eiskalt, unter Null*	In the desert the nights are often freezing cold.	
garbage [AE]	*Müll*	Tourists who come to Yellowstone are told not to leave any garbage.	= rubbish
global warming	*Erwärmung der Erde, Erderwärmung*	People today know about the dangers of global warming.	
greenhouse effect	*Treibhauseffekt*	The earth is getting warmer. Is this the greenhouse effect?	

vocabulary	dt. Bedeutung	English sentence	syn/opp
greenhouse gases	*Treibhausgase*	Millions of cars produce greenhouse gases.	
ground	*Boden*	In northern Canada the ground is frozen most of the year.	= soil, earth
hill	*Hügel, Berg, Hang*	We made an excursion into the green hills of Wales.	
hygiene	*Hygiene*	Hygiene standards in Third World countries are low.	
industrial waste	*Industrieabfall*	In the past, some countries threw their industrial waste into the North Sea.	
junk	*Müll, Abfall*	Ed's room is filled with junk.	= litter, waste, rubbish, garbage
lake	*See*	Loch Ness is the longest lake in Scotland.	
level	*Niveau; Ebene; Bereich*	A high level of ozone in the air is unhealthy.	
litter	*Abfall, Abfälle*	Do not leave litter in the countryside. Take it home with you.	= junk, waste, rubbish, garbage
(to) load	*belasten; Last*	The air in the city centres is loaded with dangerous chemicals.	
(to) melt	*schmelzen*	The ice of the poles is melting.	≠ (to) freeze
mountain	*Berg*	Even in the mountains people throw away their rubbish.	
natural gas	*Erdgas*	Natural gas was found on some Indian reservations.	
nature	*Natur*	We need nature – nature doesn't need us.	

vocabulary	dt. Bedeutung	English sentence	syn/opp
nuclear power plant	*Atomkraftwerk*	In 1986 a Soviet nuclear power plant at Chernobyl exploded.	= power station
nuclear waste	*Atommüll*	We have to find a safe place for nuclear waste.	
ocean	*Ozean*	The world's oceans are: the Atlantic, Pacific, Indian, Arctic, and Antarctic ocean.	
ozone layer	*Ozonschicht*	The ozone layer is getting thinner over the Antarctic.	
(to) persuade	*jmdn. überzeugen (etwas zu tun), überreden*	People should be persuaded to use paper bags instead of plastic ones.	
petrol [BE]	*Benzin*	Big cars use too much petrol.	= gas [AE]
(to) plant plant	*pflanzen* *Pflanze*	Let us plant more trees to keep the air fresh.	
(to) pollute	*verschmutzen*	The burning of coal and oil pollutes the air.	≠ (to) clean
polluting	*umweltschädlich*	Why don't we use the energy from the sun? It is less polluting.	
pollution	*Verschmutzung*	In the 1950s nobody thought about pollution.	
power station	*Kraftwerk*	A fire broke out at the Russian power station at Chernobyl.	
(to) protect	*schützen*	Always wear a hat to protect yourself from the sun in hot countries.	= (to) shelter
rain	*Regen*	In Scotland you get a lot of rain even in the summer.	
rain forests	*Regenwälder*	Tropical rain forests cover 7 % of the Earth's surface.	

vocabulary	dt. Bedeutung	English sentence	syn/opp
(to) recycle	*recyceln, wieder aufbereiten*	Special firms recycle bottles, plastic and paper.	
resources	*Bodenschätze, Ressourcen, Mittel,*	Coal, oil and wood are natural resources.	
return bottle	*Mehrwegflasche*	a bottle which you return to the shop so that it can be used again	
river	*Fluss, Strom*	The Missouri River is the largest river in the USA.	
rock	*(großer) Stein, Fels*	Tourists travel to the Australian outback to see Ayers Rock.	
rough	*rau, grob*	The weather in Iceland is often rough.	≠ mild
rubbish	*Abfall, Müll*	Don't leave rubbish in the countryside.	= junk, waste, garbage
(to) save	*sparen; retten*	Think about how you could save electricity.	≠ (to) waste
season	*Jahreszeit*	After the rainy season the weather gets hotter every day in India.	
(to) smell	*riechen*	Tourists who go to visit Fresh Kills dump on Staten Island can smell it before they see it!	
smoke	*Rauch*	In the 1950s the air in London was often full of thick black smoke.	
solar energy	*Sonnenenergie*	In the future, men will use more solar energy.	
solar system	*Sonnensystem*	The Earth is different from all the other planets in our solar system.	

vocabulary	dt. Bedeutung	English sentence	syn/opp
species	*Art*	Thousands of species of plants and animals could die out because of global warming.	
stream	*Bach*	The little stream behind our house is full of interesting frogs and insects.	
(to) survive	*überleben*	People need water, oxygen and food to survive.	≠ (to) die out
temperature	*Temperatur*	There are gases in the air that control the earth's temperature.	
throw-away	*Wegwerf-*	We live in a throw-away society.	
toxic waste	*Giftmüll*	Where shall we put our toxic waste?	
warning	*Warnung, Vorwarnung*	Every cigarette packet has a warning on it.	
(to) waste waste	*verschwenden* *Abfall*	Don't waste energy. Some large firms have not done much about waste yet.	≠ (to) save, (to) conserve
waste paper	*Altpapier*	Waste paper is a valuable raw material.	
waste separation	*Mülltrennung*	Germans are good at waste separation.	
waste water	*Abwasser*	Waste water must not flow into our rivers.	
weather	*Wetter*	The weather can change very quickly in this area.	
wind energy	*Windenergie*	We will need more wind energy when oil runs out.	
woods	*(kleiner) Wald*	I want to live in a house in the country with woods and open fields around it.	= forest

Europe

vocabulary	dt. Bedeutung	English sentence	syn/opp
(to) adopt	*annehmen, übernehmen*	Greece adopted the euro in 2002.	
(to) allow	*erlauben, etwas tun dürfen*	A new law allows people to live and work in many countries in Europe.	= (to) permit
(to) belong	*gehören (zu), angehören*	27 countries belonged to the European Union in 2010.	= (to) be part of
below	*unter, unten*	From the top of the Eiffel tower we looked down over the city of Paris below.	≠ above
border	*Grenze*	Illegal immigrants wanted to cross the border into Poland.	= frontier
campaign	*Werbefeldzug, Wahlkampf*	The EU started a campaign for cleaner beaches in Europe.	
century	*Jahrhundert*	We hope the 21st century will be more peaceful than the 20th century.	
ceremony	*Feier, Zeremonie*	In a ceremony five new EU members were welcomed.	
(to) complain complaint	*sich beschweren* *Beschwerde*	Some countries complained that they didn't get enough financial support.	
control (to) control	*Kontrolle* *kontrollieren, regulieren*	There is less control today at European borders.	
cooperation	*Zusammenarbeit*	Cooperation between European countries is getting better.	

vocabulary	dt. Bedeutung	English sentence	syn/opp
currency	*Währung*	16 European countries have the same currency.	
custom	*Sitte, Brauch*	All countries want to keep their customs and traditions.	
election (to) elect	*Wahl* *wählen*	An election to the European parliament takes places every four years.	
emergency	*Notfall*	Every country has special laws for an emergency.	
enemy	*Feind*	The enemies of the Second World War became friends.	≠ friend
(to) enlarge	*vergrößern*	Over the years the European Union has become enlarged.	
enterprise	*Unternehmertum, Unternehmen*	The countries of the western world believe in free enterprise.	
euro	*Euro*	16 countries of the EU now use the same money: the euro.	
European Union	*Europäische Union*	What do you know about the history of the European Union (EU)?	
exchange	*Austausch, Austauschprogramm*	This year teachers and students from my school take part in an exchange with France.	
(to) export	*exportieren, ausführen* *Ausfuhr, Export*	Germany exports a lot of machines and cars.	≠ (to) import
extract	*Auszug*	We read an extract from an article about studying in the EU.	= excerpt, passage

vocabulary	dt. Bedeutung	English sentence	syn/opp
foreign foreigner	*ausländisch* *Ausländer(in)*	Do we need more foreign workers?	= from abroad, alien
form	*Formular*	If you want to work in another EU country you do not have to fill in so many forms as in the past.	
future	*Zukunft*	In the near future more countries will join the European Union.	≠ past
government (to) govern	*Regierung* *regieren*	The government must help people who cannot find work.	
(to) guard	*bewachen*	The coasts and borders of the EU are guarded day and night.	= (to) control
head of state	*Staatsoberhaupt*	The heads of state of 27 European countries met in Brussels.	
illegal	*ungesetzlich, rechtswidrig*	It is illegal to enter the European Union without documents.	≠ legal, lawful
(to) import	*einführen* *Einfuhr*	Germany imports bananas from Central and South America.	≠ (to) export
(to) join	*beitreten, mitmachen*	The United Kingdom joined the EU in 1973.	= (to) leave
legislative	*Legislative, gesetzgebende Gewalt*	The European parliament in Strasbourg is the legislative of the EU.	
majority	*Mehrheit*	The majority of people in the EU want to live in peace.	≠ minority
(to) make a difference	*etw. bewirken*	It does make a difference if you go to vote in an election or not.	

vocabulary	dt. Bedeutung	English sentence	syn/opp
(to) make a speech	*eine Rede halten*	The British Prime Minister made a speech on the EU's foreign policy.	
market	*Markt*	The European countries created a common market.	
meeting	*Versammlung, Besprechung, Treffen*	The next meeting of European ministers will be in Vienna.	= conference
member state	*Mitgliedsstaat*	The member states of the EU work together in many areas.	
migration	*(Völker-) Wanderung*	The migration of workers from Eastern European countries to the West worries many people in Germany.	
minimum wage	*Mindestlohn*	The minimum wage is often not enough to live on.	
nationality	*Nationalität, Staatsbürger-schaft*	Simon has two nationalities: he has a German and a British passport.	
parliament	*Parlament*	The European parliament has its seat in Strasbourg.	
(to) pass a law	*ein Gesetz verabschieden*	The European parliament passed a new law on immigration.	
platform	*Parteiprogramm, Wahlplattform*	The platform of the party promises more work for all.	= programme
population (to) populate	*Bevölkerung, Einwohner (-zahl)*	Great Britain has a population of about 60, the USA of about 290 and Germany of about 82 million.	

vocabulary	dt. Bedeutung	English sentence	syn/opp
power	*Macht, Gewalt*	In the EU some countries have more power than others.	= strength ≠ weakness
probably	*wahrscheinlich*	Anne has probably found an interesting job in Malta.	
(to) protest **protest**	*protestieren* *Protest*	Farmer protested against the low price of milk.	
public	*öffentlich; Öffentlichkeit*	In many countries smoking is not allowed in public places.	≠ private
reason	*Grund*	The main reason why people left Europe for America in the 19th century was for a better life.	
refugee **refugee camp**	*Flüchtling* *Flüchtlingslager*	People who escape from war are often taken to a refugee camp first.	
regional	*regional*	There are a lot of regional differences in Europe.	
(to) remark	*anmerken, bemerken*	The headmaster remarked that three pupils would take part in an exchange with England next year.	
ruler	*Herrscher(in)*	In the 19th century the British were rulers in many parts of the world.	
session	*Sitzung, Sitzungsperiode*	The next session of the European Council will be in Cardiff.	= meeting, conference
(to) slow down	*verringern, verlangsamen*	A new law slowed down the immigration of people to Britain.	≠ (to) speed up
(to) solve	*lösen*	When countries work together they can solve many problems.	

vocabulary	dt. Bedeutung	English sentence	syn/opp
state	*Staat*	Today there are 27 states in the European Union.	= nation, country
steel	*Stahl*	The European Union began with a common market for the production and trade of coal and steel.	
straight	*direkt, geradewegs*	Sophie went to France to train as a cook straight after school.	
(to) take care of	*sich um etw. kümmern, für etw. Sorge tragen*	An au pair girl from Germany takes care of the children of the Nash family.	= (to) look after
tolerance	*Duldsamkeit, Duldung*	People should show more tolerance towards people from foreign countries.	≠ intolerance
tolerant	*duldsam*		≠ intolerant
town hall	*Rathaus*	The exchange students received a warm welcome at the town hall.	
trade	*Handel, Handelsverkehr*	Trade between EU countries has increased a lot.	
treaty	*Vertrag*	In 1992, the Treaty of Maastricht was Maastricht was signed.	
union	*Union; Gewerkschaft*	The United Kingdom and the Republic of Ireland are two countries in the European Union.	
(to) vote	*abstimmen Abstimmung*	When you are 18 you have the right to vote.	
war	*Krieg*	After the Second World War many parts of Europe were destroyed.	≠ peace
work permit	*Arbeitserlaubnis*	If you want to work in England you do not need a work permit today.	

Great Britain

vocabulary	dt. Bedeutung	English sentence	syn/opp
accent	*Akzent*	Many people find it difficult to understand the Scottish accent.	
(to) accept	*annehmen, akzeptieren*	All shops accept credit cards.	≠ (to) refuse
airport	*Flughafen*	London-Heathrow is Britain's busiest international airport.	
badge	*Abzeichen, Button*	My friend Colin wears a t-shirt with the badge of Manchester United.	
ballot	*Wahl*	A secret ballot was taken in parliament.	= vote
ballot paper	*Stimmzettel, Wahlzettel*	On a ballot paper you put a cross next to the party you vote for.	
(to) ban	*verbannen, verbieten*	In Britain, smoking is banned in restaurants.	≠ (to) allow
basic	*grundlegend*	Before we went on our trip to Wales we got some basic information about Caernarfon Castle.	
(to) be in favour of	*für etw. sein; zugunsten*	Are you in favour of or against school uniforms?	≠ (to) be against
bed and breakfast	*Übernachtung mit Frühstück*	We stayed at a B&B (bed and breakfast) in Inverness for two nights.	
(to) believe	*glauben*	Most British parents believe that their children watch too much television.	

vocabulary	dt. Bedeutung	English sentence	syn/opp
bench	*(Garten-, Park-) Bank*	We sat on a bench in Hyde Park.	
(to) book	*buchen*	I booked my holiday in Wales at the last minute.	= (to) reserve
booking	*Reservierung*	The hotel manager is happy about the number of bookings for the summer months.	= reservation
(to) camp camping	*zelten, lagern* *Camping, Zelten*	Sandra and her friends went camping in the Lake District.	
camp(ing) site	*Campingplatz*	The camp sites in Cornwall were full of French tourists.	= camping ground [AE]
camping van	*Wohnmobil*	Mr and Mrs Taylor have bought a camping van.	
capital	*Hauptstadt*	The capital of Scotland is Edinburgh, although Glasgow is the biggest city.	
(to) check in	*anmelden*	We checked in at our hotel in the afternoon.	≠ (to) check out
Catholic	*Katholik(in)*	There are more Protestants in Northern Ireland than Catholics.	
charity	*Wohltätigkeit; Wohltätigkeitsverein*	Oxfam is a British charity organisation.	
clerk	*Angestellte, Angestellter*	Thousands of bank clerks travel to work on the underground each day.	
(to) comment	*sich zu etw. äußern, einen Kommentar abgeben*	People in Britain always comment on the weather.	

vocabulary	dt. Bedeutung	English sentence	syn/opp
commentary	*Kommentar*	Every Monday I read the sports commentaries in the newspaper.	
Conservatives	*Konservative Partei*	Margaret Thatcher belonged to the Conservative Party.	
crash helmet	*Sturzhelm*	All motorcyclists must wear crash helmets.	
(to) demon-strate demonstration	*demonstrieren*	People demonstrated against the violence in Northern Ireland.	
distant distance	*entfernt, fern* *Entfernung*	In Britain the sea is never very distant. It is only 71 miles to the sea from Birmingham.	= far away ≠ near
district	*Gebiet, Bezirk*	Brixton is a district in South London where many black people live.	
(to) drive a car	*Auto fahren*	You have to pay to drive a car into central London.	
driving licence	*Führerschein*	My father has had his driving licence for more than thirty years.	
driving school	*Fahrschule*	Liz had lessons at the local driving school before she took her test.	
driving test	*Fahrprüfung*	In Britain you can take your driving test at 17.	
Empire	*das britische Weltreich, Kolonialreich*	The British Empire included Canada, Australia, New Zealand, India and large parts of Africa.	

vocabulary	dt. Bedeutung	English sentence	syn/opp
explorer	*Entdeckungs-reisender, Forscher*	James Cook was a British sailor and one of the greatest of all explorers.	
gift shop	*Geschenkartikel-laden*	We stopped at the gift shop to buy some souvenirs of London.	
government (to) govern	*Regierung* *regieren*	The prime minister is the head of the British government.	
guide (to) guide	*Reiseführer* *führen, leiten*	In London our guide told us everything about the Great Fire of 1666.	
holiday job	*Ferienarbeit*	Zoe took a holiday job in a restaurant in Stratford upon Avon.	
holiday resort	*Ferienort*	Bournemouth is a popular holiday resort on the south coast of England.	
host/hostess	*Gastgeber/ Gastgeberin*	After our stay at the house of the Brandon family we wrote a thank-you-letter to our hosts.	≠ guest
host family	*Gastfamilie*	Au pair girl Simone was very happy in her English host family.	
inhabitant (to) inhabit	*Einwohner* *bewohnen*	The Celts were the first inhabitants of the British isles.	
(to) invent invention	*erfinden* *Erfindung*	The steam engine was invented in England.	
island	*Insel*	The Isle of Wight is an island on the south coast of England.	
jail	*Gefängnis*	The Tower of London was used as a jail.	= prison

vocabulary	dt. Bedeutung	English sentence	syn/opp
journey	*Reise*	The journey from Aberdeen in Scotland to London takes 7 hours on the fastest train.	= trip
Labour Party	*Arbeiterpartei*	In the last elections, the Labour Party lost a lot of seats in the British parliament.	
landmark	*Wahrzeichen*	Big Ben is one of London's most famous landmarks.	= sight
(to) meet s.o.	*jmdn. treffen*	The prime minister meets the Queen every week to talk about the work of the government.	
Member of Parliament	*Parlaments-abgeordnete(r)*	In Britain there are more than 600 Members of Parliament.	
(to) mind I don't mind	*ausmachen* *es macht mir nichts aus*	 I didn't mind wearing a school uniform.	
minister	*Minister*	The minister said, "All school children have to take more tests."	
monarchy	*Monarchie*	Most people in Britain want to keep the monarchy.	≠ republic
nationality	*Nationalität*	Marc has double nationality: he has a German and a British passport.	
official	*offiziell*	The official language in Great Britain is English.	≠ unofficial, inofficial
once	*einst, einmal*	Ralph once worked for an American hotel group in London.	

vocabulary	dt. Bedeutung	English sentence	syn/opp
originally origin	*ursprünglich* *Ursprung, Herkunft*	The bridges in London across the river Thames were originally made of wood.	
(to) pack	*packen, einpacken*	Pack a lot of warm clothes when you go on holiday in Scotland.	≠ (to) unpack
(to) pass a law	*ein Gesetz verabschieden*	Parliament passed a new law on immigration.	
peace agreement	*Friedensab-kommen*	People hope the Peace Agreement in Northern Ireland will end the violence.	≠ war
peaceful peace	*friedlich* *Friede*	We enjoyed the peaceful countryside in North Wales.	
platform	*Bahnsteig*	The next train for Brighton leaves from platform 2.	
(to) point out	*hinweisen auf; betonen*	The guide pointed out the most important sights of London.	
politician	*Politiker(in)*	Most politicians are members of a political party.	
politics political	*Politik, Staatskunst* *politisch*	Are you interested in politics?	
power	*Macht, Gewalt*	Who came to power in the last British elections?	
prime minister	*Premier-minister(in)*	Margaret Thatcher (1979 – 1990) was the first woman to become prime minister.	
public	*Öffentlichkeit, öffentlich*	Buckingham Palace is open to the public from July to September.	

vocabulary	dt. Bedeutung	English sentence	syn/opp
public holiday	*gesetzlicher Feiertag*	December 25, Christmas Day, is a public holiday in Britain.	
public transport	*öffentliche Verkehrmittel*	Public transport in London is very expensive.	
queue	*(Warte-) Schlange*	There is a long queue in front of the London Eye.	
regional	*regional*	Britain has a large number of regional papers.	≠ national
royal	*königlich*	Many people are interested in the latest news about the British royal family.	
rush-hour	*Hauptverkehrs-zeit*	If you want to go into the centre of London try not to travel during the rush-hour.	
seaside resort	*Seebad*	We always spend our holidays at the seaside resort Torquay.	
seat belt	*Sicherheitsgurt*	In Britain, all car drivers must wear seat belts.	
single room	*Einzelzimmer*	I booked a single room for two weeks at the Red Lion pub in Keswick.	
(to) slow down	*verringern, verlangsamen*	The Immigration Law of 1971 slowed down immigration to Britain.	≠ (to) speed up
(to) spend	*verbringen*	I would like to spend Christmas in the Scottish Highlands.	

vocabulary	dt. Bedeutung	English sentence	syn/opp
town hall	*Rathaus*	The sportsmen who had won an Olympic medal for Great Britain were invited to a party in the town hall.	
traffic	*Verkehr*	Big cities such as London have a lot of traffic problems.	
traffic sign	*Verkehrszeichen*	The Romans put up the first traffic signs in Britain.	
vegetarian	*Vegetarier(in)*	There are lots of restaurants in London for vegetarians.	
vehicle	*Fahrzeug*	No vehicles are allowed into the city centre between 8 a.m. and 6 p.m.	
village	*Dorf*	Terry lives with his parents and his younger sister in a village in Wales.	

USA

vocabulary	dt. Bedeutung	English sentence	syn/opp
advantage	*Vorteil*	It is an advantage for children of Mexican families to learn to speak English early.	≠ disadvantage
African Americans Afro-Americans	*Afroamerikaner*	Today, black people in the USA are called 'African Americans' or 'Afro-Americans'.	
arrive	*ankommen, eintreffen*	The first Europeans arrived in America in 1492.	≠ (to) leave, (to) depart
arrival	*Ankunft*		≠ departure
attraction	*Anziehung, Touristen-attraktion*	Universal Studios in Los Angeles is a very popular tourist attraction.	
(to) attract	*anziehen*		
battle	*Schlacht, Kampf*	Sitting Bull was one of the Sioux chiefs at the battle of Little Bighorn in 1876.	
beach	*Strand*	California has some great beaches – for example Venice Beach in L. A.	
belt	*Gürtel*	Parts of the South, Southwest, and West are sometimes called the Sun Belt because the sun shines a lot there.	
on board	*an Bord*	The Pilgrim Fathers arrived in 1620 on board the Mayflower.	
cab [AE]	*Taxi*	Many cab drivers in New York are from Asia, especially Pakistan.	= taxi [BE]

vocabulary	dt. Bedeutung	English sentence	syn/opp
candy [AE]	*Süßigkeiten, Bonbons*	Most American kids like candy, but it's not good for their teeth.	= sweets [BE]
capital	*Hauptstadt*	The capital of the USA is Washington, D.C.	
cargo	*Ladung, Fracht*	In Boston a group of colonists threw a cargo of tea into the harbour.	
(to) celebrate	*feiern*	Americans celebrate Independence Day on July 4th.	
celebration	*Feier*	Independence Day is a very patriotic celebration.	
chief	*Häuptling*	Geronimo was an Indian chief of the Apache.	
college	*Hochschule (in den USA)*	Sally told her parents that she wanted to go to college.	
colony	*Kolonie*	Until 1819 Florida was a Spanish colony.	
comfortable	*bequem*	Our seats on the plane to Boston were very comfortable.	≠ uncomfortable
community	*Gemeinde, Gemeinschaft*	The Mormons are a religious community in Utah.	
(to) contribute	*etwas zu etw. beisteuern*	The immigrants contributed to the richness of America.	
(to) cover	*bedecken*	Disneyland covers 20 square kilometres, an area as big as one fifth of Paris.	≠ (to) discover

vocabulary	dt. Bedeutung	English sentence	syn/opp
credit card	*Kreditkarte*	In the USA credit cards are accepted in almost all shops and restaurants.	
crime	*Verbrechen*	There's a lot of crime in many big cities of the United States.	
crowded	*(mit Menschen) überfüllt*	In the summer, the streets, shops and restaurants in New York are crowded with tourists.	
culture	*Kultur*	The whites destroyed many native American cultures.	
department	*Ministerium, Abteilung*	The US government departments are in Washington, D.C.	
desert	*Wüste*	Some southern parts of the Rocky Mountains are dry stony deserts.	
disease	*Krankheit*	President Ronald Reagan developed Alzheimer's disease after he left office.	= illness ≠ health
(to) disguise	*sich verkleiden*	At Halloween (October 31st) children in the USA disguise themselves as ghosts, witches or monsters.	
downtown	*das Zentrum, die Innenstadt*	When we arrived in San Francisco we took a cable car downtown.	
dry	*trocken*	In the Midwest, there is less rainfall and the grass looks dry.	≠ wet
elevator	*Fahrstuhl, Aufzug*	The elevators in the Empire State building take tourists to the top floor.	

vocabulary	dt. Bedeutung	English sentence	syn/opp
entrance (to) enter	*Eingang, Zugang* *eintreten*	The Statue of Liberty stands at the entrance to New York harbour.	
ethnic group	*Volksgruppe*	Many different ethnic groups live in the United States of America.	
exciting	*aufregend, spannend*	A trip on the Colorado River in a rubber dinghy is an exciting and sometimes dangerous adventure.	≠ boring
fall [AE]	*Herbst*	The American word for the British word "autumn" is "fall".	= autumn [BE]
farming	*Landwirtschaft*	In the US, farming has always been very important.	
flag	*Fahne, Flagge*	All American schools have an American flag in their classrooms.	
flight (to) fly	*Flug* *fliegen*	During our flight to Chicago we ate two meals and we watched a film.	
freedom	*Freiheit*	President Abraham Lincoln fought for freedom for slaves.	≠ slavery
gas, gasoline [AE]	*Benzin*	Gas is rather cheap in the USA.	= petrol [BE]
geography	*Erdkunde, Geographie*	In the geography lesson, the students learned about wildlife in Alaska.	
grape	*Weintraube*	Sue went picking grapes in California.	

vocabulary	dt. Bedeutung	English sentence	syn/opp
highway, freeway [AE]	*Fernstraße*	Many tourists travel on the famous old highway Route 66, which runs from Chicago to Los Angeles.	= motorway [BE]
Hispanic	*Hispano-Amerikaner(in); spanischsprachig*	Hispanic people come from Latin American countries such as Mexico, Costa Rica or Panama. They speak Spanish.	
immigrant	*Einwanderer*	Immigrants from all over the world brought their religion, their music and their culture to the USA.	≠ emigrant
immigration	*Einwanderung*	Today Ellis Island is a museum about immigration.	≠ emigration
(to) improve	*verbessern, vorankommen*	Most people who went to America wanted to improve their living conditions.	
independence	*Unabhängigkeit*	July 4th is Independence Day, the birthday of the United States of America.	≠ dependence
independent	*unabhängig*	The colonies in North America became independent as "The United States of America" in 1776.	≠ dependent
Indian	*Indianer(in)*	After the Indian Wars were over in 1890, white Americans moved the Indians to reservations.	
institution	*Einrichtung*	Harvard University is an institution which is famous for its excellent students.	

vocabulary	dt. Bedeutung	English sentence	syn/opp
interstate	*Autobahn (durch mehrere US-Bundesstaaten)*	The speed limit on the interstate in Arizona is 75 mph (miles per hour).	
lake	*See*	Lakes Superior, Michigan, Huron, Erie, and Ontario - the five Great Lakes – are the world's largest group of freshwater lakes.	
law	*Gesetz*	Each state of the US has its own government and makes its own laws.	
liberty	*Freiheit*	The Statue of Liberty was a present of the French people to the Americans.	= freedom
limit	*Grenze*	The speed limit on American highways is between 45 and 75 mph (miles per hour).	
minority	*Minderheit*	Hispanics are the largest minority group in the USA.	≠ majority
mixed	*gemischt*	In the US many mixed cultures live side by side.	
movie [AE]	*Film*	How often have you seen the movie "Titanic"?	= film [BE]
national park	*Nationalpark*	Yellowstone national park was officially opened in 1872.	
native	*einheimisch*	At some schools children of immigrants are taught in English and their native language.	
Native Americans	*Indianer in den USA*	Native Americans have lived in the Grand Canyon region for many centuries.	

vocabulary	dt. Bedeutung	English sentence	syn/opp
neighborhood [AE]	*Viertel, Nachbarschaft*	You have to be careful in some neighborhoods of New York.	= neighbour-hood [BE]
noisy	*laut, geräuschvoll*	Times Square in New York is a noisy place.	≠ quiet
origin	*Ursprung*	In the 19th century most immigrants were of European origin.	
president	*Präsident*	The President lives in the White House in Washington, D. C.	
pride (to) take pride in	*Stolz* *stolz sein auf*	Americans take pride in their country's history and traditions.	
(to) protect protection	*schützen* *Schutz*	National parks help to protect animals and plants.	= (to) save
Puritans	*Puritaner*	In 1620, the Puritans sailed from England to America on the Mayflower.	
race	*Rennen*	The Kentucky Derby is the most famous American horse race.	
race	*Rasse*	Different races are living together in the same district.	
railroad, railway	*Eisenbahn*	The railroad across the American continent was completed in 1869.	
(to) rent	*mieten, leihen*	In Los Angeles we rented a car to drive around California and Arizona.	=(to) hire
reservation (to) reserve	*Reservierung, Buchung* *buchen*	We made a reservation because we knew that the hotel would be full.	= booking = (to) book

vocabulary	dt. Bedeutung	English sentence	syn/opp
(to) retire	*in Pension gehen, in Rente gehen*	A lot of older people retire to Florida or Arizona, because it is warmer there.	
route	*Route, Strecke*	The Mississippi River is an important transportation route for agricultural and industrial products.	
(to) sail	*in See stechen, auslaufen*	The Pilgrim Fathers sailed from Plymouth (England) to the New World.	
security	*Sicherheit, Sicherheits-vorkehrungen*	When you want to fly to the USA you have to go through several security checks at the airport.	
secure	*sicher*		= safe ≠ dangerous
(to) settle	*sich niederlassen, siedeln*	The English first settled on the east coast of the American continent.	
settler	*Siedler*	The white settlers killed many buffaloes.	
sight (to) see	*Sehenswürdigkeit* *sehen*	Golden Gate Bridge is one of the well-known sights of San Francisco.	= landmark
(to) sign	*unterzeichnen, unterschreiben*	The white general and the Indian chief signed a peace treaty.	
site	*Ort, Platz*	Niagara Falls is one of the most beautiful natural sites in North America.	
skyscraper	*Wolkenkratzer*	The world's first skyscraper was built in Chicago in 1885.	
slave	*Sklave*	Millions of blacks worked as slaves on the farms in the American south.	

vocabulary	dt. Bedeutung	English sentence	syn/opp
snack food	*Kleinigkeit zum Naschen, Knabberzeug*	Chocolate, candy and crisps are snack foods.	
snake	*Schlange*	Wild animals – bears, snakes and wolves – live in Yellowstone park.	
southern	*südlich, Süd*	Mississippi is a state in the southern part of the USA.	≠ northern
space	*Raum, Platz*	The USA is a huge country with a lot of space.	
spectacular	*atemberaubend, fantastisch*	From the top of the Empire State building you have a spectacular view of the city of New York.	
standard of living	*Lebensstandard*	Most Americans enjoy a high standard of living.	
Statue of Liberty	*Freiheitsstatue*	The Statue of Liberty in New York is 93.5 metres high.	
steep	*steil*	We climbed a steep mountain in Colorado.	
store	*Laden, Geschäft*	Campers can buy food at the local camp store.	= shop
subway [AE]	*U-Bahn*	The German tourists took the subway to Greenwich Village.	= underground [BE]
teenage curfew, teen curfew	*Ausgangssperre für Teenager*	Teenage curfew is a law which does not allow teenagers to be on the streets after 10 o'clock at night.	

vocabulary	dt. Bedeutung	English sentence	syn/opp
Thanksgiving	*amerikanisches Erntedankfest*	Thanksgiving (the fourth Thursday in November) is a public holiday, when families come together for a long weekend.	
traffic jam	*(Verkehrs-) Stau*	On our drive to Los Angeles we got stuck in a traffic jam for two hours.	
traveller's cheque	*Reisescheck*	When you go shopping in an American supermarket you can pay by traveller's cheque.	
tribe	*(Volks-) Stamm*	Before white people came to America, Indian tribes like the Sioux crossed the country and hunted buffaloes for clothes, tents and food.	
turkey	*Truthahn, -henne*	At Thanksgiving most people have a turkey dinner.	
vacation [AE]	*Ferien*	We enjoyed our spring vacation in Nevada.	= holiday [BE]
(to) wound	*verwunden, verletzen*	In the American Civil War thousands died in battles and many more were wounded.	

Grundwortschatz

able	*etwas tun können, fähig sein*
about	*über; ungefähr*
above	*über, oberhalb*
abroad	*ins, im Ausland*
accent	*Akzent*
(to) accept	*annehmen*
accident	*Unfall*
accommodation	*Unterkunft*
across	*über (… hinweg)*
(to) act	*handeln, sich verhalten*
action	*Handeln*
active	*aktiv, lebhaft*
activity	*Tätigkeit, Beschäftigung*
actual	*eigentlich, tatsächlich*
actually	*eigentlich*
(to) add	*zusammenzählen*
(to) address	*ansprechen*
advantage	*Vorteil*
adventure	*Abenteuer*
(to) advertise	*werben für*
advertising	*Werbung, Reklame*
advice	*Rat (-schlag)*
(to) advise	*beraten, jmdm. raten*
afraid	*verängstigt*
afternoon	*Nachmittag*
against	*gegen*
age	*Alter*
ago	*vor*
(to) agree	*übereinstimmen*
agreement	*Vereinbarung*
ahead	*vorn, in Führung*
air	*Luft*
alcohol	*Alkohol*
alive	*lebendig, (noch) am Leben*
(to) allow	*erlauben, ermöglichen*
almost	*fast, beinah*
alone	*allein*
along	*vorwärts*
already	*schon, bereits*
also	*auch, ebenfalls, außerdem*
although	*obwohl, obgleich*
always	*immer, ständig*
angry	*zornig*

animal	*Tier*
answer	*Antwort*
anybody	*jemand*
anything	*alles*
apart	*getrennt, für sich*
application	*Bewerbung*
(to) apply for	*sich bewerben um*
apprentice	*Lehrling, Auszubildender*
(to) argue	*argumentieren, sich aussprechen für*
(to) argue	*sich streiten, Einwendungen machen*
arm	*Arm*
(to) arrive	*ankommen*
art	*(bildende) Kunst*
as far as	*so weit*
(to) ask	*fragen*
(to) ask for	*bitten*
assistant	*stellvertretende(r, s), Assistent, Gehilfe*
at last	*endlich*
at least	*wenigstens*
at night	*nachts*
at school	*in der Schule*
attractive	*attraktiv, anziehend*

autumn	*Herbst*
average	*Durchschnitt*
awake	*aufwachen, erwachen*
away	*weg*
back	*zurück*
bad	*schlecht, schlimm*
badly	*schlecht; sehr, dringend*
bag	*Tasche*
band	*Band, Gruppe*
bank	*Bank; Ufer*
bar	*Stange, Riegel*
basic	*grundlegend, fundamental, einfach*
bathroom	*Badezimmer*
battery	*Batterie*
battle	*Schlacht*
(to) be able to	*können*
(to) be going to	*werden*
(to) be in love with	*lieben, verliebt sein in*
beautiful	*schön*
(to) become	*werden*
before	*vor*
(to) begin	*anfangen*
(to) behave	*sich benehmen*

behaviour	*Verhalten, Benehmen*
behind	*hinten, dahinter, zurück*
(to) believe in	*glauben an*
(to) belong to	*angehören, Mitglied sein in*
below	*unten, unter*
belt	*Gürtel*
bench	*(Park-, Garten-) Bank*
bend	*Kurve*
(to) bend down	*sich bücken*
(to) bet	*wetten*
between	*zwischen*
birth	*Geburt*
birthday	*Geburtstag*
bit	*Stückchen, Stück*
(to) blame	*die Schuld geben, beschuldigen*
blind	*blind*
block	*Block, Holzklotz*
block of flats	*Wohnhaus, Mietshaus*
(to) blow	*wehen, blasen*
blue	*blau, traurig, deprimiert*
board	*Brett, Tafel*
boat	*Boot, Schiff*
body	*Körper*
booking	*Reservierung*
border	*Grenze*
bored	*gelangweilt*
boring	*langweilig*
born	*geboren*
(to) borrow	*borgen, ausleihen*
both	*beide*
bound	*Verpflichtung, Belastung*
bowl	*Schale, Schüssel, Napf*
brain	*Gehirn, Verstand, Intelligenz*
(to) brake	*bremsen*
branch	*Zweig; Filiale, Zweigstelle*
(to) break	*brechen*
breakfast	*Frühstück*
bridge	*Brücke*
bright	*hell*
(to) bring up	*aufziehen, großziehen*
broken	*zerbrochen*
brother	*Bruder*
brown	*braun*
(to) brush	*bürsten, putzen; Bürste*
building	*Gebäude*

(to) burn	*brennen, verbrennen*
(to) burst	*brechen*
bus	*Omnibus, Schulbus*
bush	*Busch, Gebüsch*
business	*Unternehmen, Geschäft, Branche*
busy	*belebt, beschäftigt*
butter	*Butter*
button	*Knopf*
(to) buy	*kaufen*
by birth	*von Geburt*
by mistake	*aus Versehen*
by trade	*von Beruf*
bye-bye	*Auf Wiedersehen*
(to) call	*rufen, nennen*
capital	*Hauptstadt*
car	*Wagen*
care	*Sorgfalt*
career	*Karriere, Laufbahn*
careful	*vorsichtig*
(to) carry	*tragen*
centre	*Mitte, Zentrum*
century	*Jahrhundert*
challenge	*Herausforderung*
chance	*Gelegenheit*
(to) change	*wechseln, tauschen*
(to) change a tyre	*einen Reifen wechseln*
(to) charge	*(Geld) verlangen; angreifen*
(to) chat	*schwätzen*
cheap	*billig, günstig*
(to) check	*kontrollieren*
(to) check in	*sich anmelden*
(to) cheer	*anfeuern*
chicken	*Huhn, Hähnchen*
chief	*oberster, wichtigster, Haupt-*
child	*Kind*
choice	*(Aus-) Wahl*
(to) choose	*wählen, aussuchen*
Christmas	*Weihnachten*
church	*Kirche*
cinema	*Kino*
circle	*Kreis*
city	*(Groß-) stadt*
class	*Kategorie*
classroom	*Klassenzimmer*
(to) clean	*putzen*
clear	*klar*
clerk	*Angestellter, Büroangestellter*
clever	*begabt*

(to) climb	*klettern*
clock	*Uhr*
(to) close	*schließen, zumachen*
close	*nahe, eng, dicht*
closed	*geschlossen, zu*
clothes	*Kleider*
club	*Klub*
coffee	*Kaffee*
cold	*kalt*
(to) collect	*sammeln, ansammeln*
colour	*Farbe*
combination	*Verkettung, Verbindung*
comfort	*Behaglichkeit; Trost*
comfortable	*bequem*
communication	*Verständigung*
company	*Unternehmen, Firma; Gesellschaft*
(to) complain	*sich beschweren, sich beklagen*
complaint	*Beschwerde, Klage*
(to) complete	*vervollständigen*
completely	*völlig*
concentration	*Konzentration*
confident	*zuversichtlich*
(to) congratulate	*beglückwünschen, gratulieren*
(to) connect	*verbinden*
connected	*verbunden sein*
constantly	*ständig, dauernd*
construction	*Bauwerk*
(to) consult	*um Rat fragen*
(to) contain	*enthalten*
(to) contribute	*etwas zu etwas beisteuern, beitragen*
control	*Kontrolle*
(to) cook	*kochen, eine Mahlzeit zubereiten*
cool	*kühl*
(to) copy	*abschreiben, kopieren*
corner	*Ecke*
(to) correct	*jmdn./etwas korrigieren*
correctly	*richtig*
(to) cost	*kosten*
(to) cough	*husten, Husten*
could	*konnte; könnte*
(to) count	*zählen*
country	*Land*
countryside	*Landschaft*
course	*Kurs, Lehrgang*
cover	*(Buch-) Einband, Deckel*

(to) cover	*bedecken; behandeln, erfassen*
(to) crash	*zusammenstoßen (mit), hineinfahren (in)*
(to) crash into	*prallen gegen*
crazy	*verrückt*
creature	*Lebewesen*
credit card	*Kreditkarte*
crime	*Verbrechen*
crisis	*Krise*
criticism	*Kritik*
cross	*Kreuz*
crowd	*Menge*
crowded	*überfüllt*
cruel	*grausam*
(to) cry	*weinen*
culture	*Kultur*
curriculum vitae (CV)	*Lebenslauf*
(to) cut	*schneiden, ausschneiden*
(to) dance	*tanzen*
dangerous	*gefährlich, gefahrvoll*
(to) dare	*jmdn. herausfordern, wagen*
dark	*dunkel, finster*
date	*Verabredung*
day	*Tag*
dead	*tot*
deaf	*taub*
(to) deal	*austeilen, handeln*
dear	*lieb, teuer*
(to) decide	*(sich) entschließen, entscheiden*
decision	*Entscheidung*
deep	*tief*
degree	*Grad*
(to) deliver	*liefern; (eine Rede) halten*
(to) describe	*beschreiben*
(to) design	*entwerfen; Entwurf*
(to) destroy	*zerstören*
detail	*Detail, Einzelheit*
(to) develop	*(sich) entwickeln*
(to) die	*sterben*
diet	*Kost, Nahrung*
difference	*Unterschied*
different	*verschieden*
dinner	*Abendessen, Abendbrot*
(to) direct	*richten*
direction	*Richtung*

(to) disagree	*nicht zustimmen*
(to) discuss	*besprechen*
dish	*Schale, Schüssel, Platte; Gericht*
dishes [Pl.]	*Geschirr*
distance	*Entfernung*
(to) divide	*teilen*
division	*Verteilung*
dole	*Arbeitslosengeld*
door	*Tür*
downstairs	*treppab, die Treppe hinunter, unten*
downtown	*Innenstadt*
(to) draw	*zeichnen; ziehen*
drawing	*Zeichnen, Zeichnung*
(to) dream	*träumen*
dream	*Traum*
(to) dress	*sich kleiden; Kleid*
(to) drink	*trinken; Getränk*
(to) drive	*fahren; Auffahrt*
driving licence	*Führerschein*
(to) drop	*fallen; Fall, Sturz*
drug	*Droge*
(to) dry	*trocknen*
during	*während*
early	*früh*
(to) earn	*(Geld) verdienen*
earth	*Erde*
easy	*leicht, einfach*
(to) eat	*essen*
education	*Erziehung, Ausbildung*
effect	*Wirkung*
election	*Wahl*
electricity	*Elektrizität*
else	*alle anderen, sonst*
embarrassed	*verlegen, peinlich berührt*
emergency	*Notfall*
emigrant	*Auswanderer(in)*
(to) emigrate	*auswandern*
emigration	*Auswanderung*
emotion	*Gefühl*
empty	*leer*
(to) encourage	*ermutigen*
end	*Ende*
enemy	*Feind*
engine	*Motor, Maschine*
(to) enjoy	*genießen*
enough	*genügend, ausreichend*
(to) enter	*betreten; einreisen in; teilnehmen an*

entertainment	*Unterhaltung*
enthusiastic	*begeistert*
entrance	*Eingang*
environment	*Umwelt*
equal	*gleich*
equipment	*Ausrüstung*
error	*Fehler*
(to) escape	*entfliehen*
especially	*besonders, insbesondere*
ethnic	*Volks-*
even	*sogar, selbst*
even (number)	*gerade (Zahl)*
event	*Ereignis*
every	*jede(r, s)*
everybody	*jede(r)*
everything	*alles*
everywhere	*überall*
exact	*genau*
exam	*Prüfung*
(to) examine	*untersuchen*
example	*Beispiel*
excellent	*ausgezeichnet*
except	*außer*
(to) exchange	*tauschen*
(to) excite	*auf-, erregen*
excited	*aufgeregt*
exciting	*aufregend*
(to) excuse	*entschuldigen*
(to) exercise	*trainieren, üben*
exhibition	*Ausstellung*
(to) exist	*existieren, bestehen*
existence	*Dasein, Leben*
(to) expect	*erwarten*
expensive	*teuer*
experience	*Erfahrung*
experienced	*erfahren*
experiment	*Versuch*
(to) explain	*erklären*
(to) explode	*explodieren*
extremely	*äußerst, außerordentlich*
eye	*Auge*
(to) face	*sich gegenübersehen*
fact	*Tatsache*
factory	*Fabrik*
(to) fail	*durchfallen (bei einer Prüfung)*
(to) fall	*fallen, stürzen*
false	*falsch*
fame	*Ruhm*
family	*Familie*

famous	*berühmt*
far	*von weit her, weit entfernt*
fashion	*Mode*
fast	*schnell*
fat	*fett*
father	*Vater*
fault	*Fehler*
favour	*Gefälligkeit*
favourite	*Lieblings-*
fear	*Angst*
(to) fear	*fürchten*
(to) feed	*ernähren, füttern*
(to) feel	*fühlen*
feeling	*Gefühl*
female	*weiblich*
ferry	*Fähre*
(to) fetch	*holen*
few	*wenig(e)*
field	*Wiese, Feld*
fight	*Kampf*
figure	*Gestalt, Zahl*
(to) fill	*füllen*
finally	*schließlich*
find	*finden*
fine	*Geldstrafe*
fine	*gut, fein, schön*
finger	*Finger*
(to) finish	*enden, aufhören*
(to) fire	*entlassen*
firm	*Firma*
first	*erste(r, s)*
(to) fit	*passen (Anzug, Kleid)*
flat	*flach*
flat	*Wohnung*
flavour	*Geschmack*
flight	*Flug*
flour	*Mehl*
(to) fly	*fliegen*
(to) follow	*folgen*
food	*Essen, Nahrung*
foot	*Fuß*
for good	*endgültig*
foreign	*ausländisch*
forest	*Wald*
forever	*für immer*
(to) forget	*vergessen*
fork	*Gabel*
(to) form	*bilden*
formal	*förmlich, formell*
fortune	*Vermögen*

forward	*nach vorn*
freak	*Fanatiker(in)*
free	*frei*
free of charge	*kostenlos*
freedom	*Freiheit*
fresh	*frisch*
friend	*Freund*
friendly	*freundlich*
(to) frighten	*jmdn. erschrecken, jmdm. Angst machen*
frightened	*verängstigt*
front	*Vorderseite*
frontier	*Grenzland, Grenze*
frustrated	*enttäuscht, unbefriedigt*
full	*voll*
fun	*Spaß*
funny	*lustig, witzig*
future	*Zukunft*
game	*Spiel*
garbage	*Müll*
gas	*Benzin [AE] BE: petrol*
gate	*Tor, Sperre; Flugsteig*
(to) gather	*sammeln*
general	*allgemein*
(to) get rid of	*los werden*
(to) get up	*aufstehen*
(to) get used to	*sich gewöhnen an*
ghost	*Geist, Gespenst*
(to) give	*geben*
(to) give a hand	*behilflich sein*
(to) give up	*aufgeben, aufhören*
glad	*froh, erfreut, freudig*
glass	*Glas*
glasses	*Brille*
goal	*Ziel, Tor*
good-bye	*Auf Wiedersehen, Lebewohl!*
(to) govern	*regieren*
government	*Regierung*
grade	*Rang, Note*
(to) grant	*gewähren, bewilligen*
grape	*(Wein-) traube*
great	*groß, großartig*
greeting	*Begrüßung, Gruß*
grey [AE], gray [BE]	*grau*
ground	*(Erd-) boden, Stadion*
group	*Gruppe*
(to) grow	*wachsen*
growth	*Wachstum*

(to) guard	*bewachen*
(to) guess	*(er-) raten, vermuten*
(to) guide	*führen, leiten*
gun	*(Schuss-) Waffe*
guy	*Typ, Bursche*
hair	*Haar*
hairdresser	*Friseur, Friseurin*
half	*halb; Hälfte*
hall	*Diele*
ham	*Schinken*
hand	*hand*
(to) handle	*handhaben, behandeln*
(to) hang	*aufhängen*
(to) happen	*sich ereignen*
hard	*hart, schwer*
hardly	*kaum*
hardware	*Eisenwaren; Computerhardware*
hate	*Hass; hassen*
(to) have	*haben*
head	*Kopf*
health	*Gesundheit*
healthy	*gesund*
(to) hear	*hören*
heart	*Herz*
heavy	*schwer*
height	*Höhe*
help	*Hilfe*
her	*sie, ihr*
hero	*Held*
herself	*sich*
high	*hoch*
himself	*sich*
(to) hire	*mieten*
history	*Geschichte*
(to) hit	*schlagen*
hold	*Halt; halten*
holiday	*Urlaub*
home	*Zuhause*
(to) hope	*hoffen*
hospital	*Krankenhaus*
hostel	*Heim, Herberge*
human	*menschlich*
hungry	*hungrig*
(to) hunt	*jagen*
(to) hurry	*sich beeilen*
(to) hurt	*verletzen*
husband	*(Ehe-) Mann*
idea	*Vorstellung*
ideal	*vorbildlich*

identity	*Identität*
(to) ignore	*nicht beachten*
ill	*krank*
illegal	*ungesetzlich, rechtswidrig*
illness	*Krankheit*
image	*Ebenbild, Bild*
imagination	*Fantasie*
(to) imagine	*sich vorstellen*
immense	*ungeheuer, unermesslich*
immigrant	*Einwanderer*
(to) immigrate	*einwandern*
immigration	*Einwanderung*
importance	*Wichtigkeit*
important	*wichtig*
impossible	*unmöglich*
(to) improve	*(sich) verbessern, vorankommen*
in favour of	*für*
(to) increase	*zunehmen, steigen*
increase	*Erhöhung, Zunahme, Steigerung*
increasing	*zunehmend, steigend*
independent	*unabhängig*
industrial	*industriell*
influence	*Einfluss*
(to) inform	*benachrichtigen*
informal	*locker*
information	*Information*
injection	*Injektion*
(to) injure	*verletzen*
injury	*Verletzung*
inside	*drinnen*
instead	*statt dessen, anstatt*
instruction	*Anweisung, Gebrauchsanweisung*
intelligent	*klug, intelligent*
interest	*Interesse; Zins*
(to) interrupt	*unterbrechen*
interview	*Vorstellungsgespräch*
(to) introduce	*(jmdn., sich) vorstellen*
invitation	*Einladung*
(to) invite	*einladen*
island	*Insel*
its	*sein, seine*
jam	*Marmelade*
job	*Stellung, Arbeitsstelle*
(to) join	*sich anschließen, beitreten, mitmachen*
joke	*Witz*
journalist	*Journalist*
journey	*Reise*

juice	*Saft*
(to) jump	*springen*
junk food	*Nahrung ohne Nährwert*
(to) keep	*(be-) halten*
key	*Schlüssel*
keyboard	*Tastatur*
(to) kick	*treten*
kid	*Kind*
(to) kill	*töten*
kind	*freundlich, liebenswürdig*
kind	*Art*
kindness	*Freundlichkeit, Liebenswürdigkeit*
kingdom	*Königreich*
kiss	*Kuss*
kitchen	*Küche*
kite	*Drachen*
knife	*Messer*
(to) knock	*klopfen*
(to) know	*wissen*
labour	*Arbeit*
lake	*(Binnen-) See*
land	*land*
language	*Sprache*
(to) last	*dauern*
at last	*endlich, schließlich*
late	*spät*
latest	*neuesten*
(to) laugh	*lachen*
law	*Gesetz*
(to) lay	*legen; (den Tisch) decken*
(to) lead	*führen*
leaf	*Blatt*
(to) learn	*lernen*
least	*am wenigsten*
(to) leave	*verlassen*
legal	*gesetzlich zulässig, legal*
(to) lend	*etw. verleihen*
less	*weniger*
lesson	*Unterrichtsstunde, Lektion*
let	*lassen, erlauben; vermieten*
lethal	*tödlich*
letter	*Brief*
level	*Höhe, Niveau*
library	*Bücherei*
licence	*Genehmigung*
life story	*Biographie*

(to) lift	*heben*
light	*leicht*
(to) limit	*begrenzen*
(to) listen	*hören (Radio)*
(to) live	*leben*
live [ai]	*direkt (TV- oder Radiosendung)*
local	*örtlich*
lock	*(Tür-) Schloss*
lonely	*einsam, allein*
(to) look forward to	*sich freuen auf*
loose	*locker*
lorry	*Lastwagen*
(to) lose	*verlieren*
loss	*Verlust*
lot	*viel*
low	*niedrig; leise (Stimme)*
lunch	*Mittagessen*
lunch time	*Mittagspause*
lungs [Pl.]	*Lunge*
machine	*Maschine*
mad	*verrückt*
magazine	*Zeitschrift*
mail	*Post*
main	*Haupt-*
mainly	*hauptsächlich*
(to) make	*machen*
(to) make a speech	*eine Rede halten*
male	*männlich*
manager	*Leiter, Direktor*
(to) march	*marschieren*
market	*Markt*
marks	*(Schul-) Noten*
marriage	*Heirat, Ehe*
married	*verheiratet*
(to) marry	*heiraten*
(to) match	*passen (farblich)*
material	*Material*
maths	*Mathe*
matter	*Angelegenheit*
(to) matter	*von Bedeutung sein*
maybe	*vielleicht*
meal	*Mahlzeit*
mean	*bedeuten*
meaning	*Sinn, Bedeutung*
means	*Mittel*
mechanic	*Mechaniker*
media	*die Medien*
(to) meet	*(sich) treffen*

meeting	*Treffen, Versammlung, Zusammenkunft*
(to) melt	*schmelzen*
member	*Mitglied*
memory	*Gedächtnis*
(to) mention	*erwähnen*
message	*Nachricht, Botschaft*
middle	*Mitte*
mind	*Sinn, Verstand*
(to) mind	*ausmachen (in Sätzen wie: Es macht mir nichts aus …)*
mine	*meine(r, s)*
mine	*Bergwerk*
minimum wage	*Mindestlohn*
minority	*Minderheit*
minute	*Minute; winzig*
(to) miss	*verpassen, vermissen*
mistake	*Fehler, Irrtum*
(to) mix	*mischen*
model	*Modell*
moment	*Augenblick*
money	*Geld*
month	*Monat*
moon	*Mond*
most	*die meisten*
mother	*Mutter*
motion	*Bewegung*
motorbike	*Motorrad*
motorcyclist	*Motorradfahrer(in)*
mouth	*Mund*
(to) move	*sich bewegen, umziehen; Bewegung, Zug*
movement	*Bewegung*
muscle	*Muskel*
musician	*Musiker*
mustn't	*darf nicht*
mysterious	*geheimnisvoll*
mystery	*Geheimnis, Rätsel*
narrow	*eng, schmal*
native	*einheimisch, (Ur-)Einwohner*
naturally	*natürlich*
nature	*Natur*
near	*nahe, in der Nähe*
nearly	*fast, beinahe*
neat	*ordentlich, sauber*
necessary	*nötig, notwendig*
need	*Bedürfnis, Bedarf; brauchen*
needn't	*brauch nicht, muss nicht*

negative	*negativ, ablehnend*
neighbourhood	*Nachbarschaft*
nephew	*Neffe*
nerve	*Nerv*
nervous	*nervös, aufgeregt, ängstlich*
news [Pl.]	*Nachrichten (-sendung)*
newspaper	*Tageszeitung*
nice	*schön, angenehm*
niece	*Nichte*
night	*Nacht*
noble	*edel, großzügig*
nobody	*niemand*
noise	*Lärm, Krach*
noisy	*laut, lärmend*
(to) nominate	*nominieren, aufstellen*
nonsense	*Unsinn*
nose	*Nase*
not yet	*noch nicht*
(to) note	*beachten*
notebook	*Notizbuch*
notes	*Notizen*
(to) notice	*jmdn./etw. bemerken*
nowhere	*nirgends, nirgendwo*
number	*Zahl*
nurse	*Krankenschwester, Krankenpfleger(in)*
object	*Objekt, Gegenstand, Ziel*
offer	*Angebot; anbieten*
office	*Büro*
official	*offiziell, amtlich*
often	*oft, häufig*
oil	*Öl*
old-fashioned	*altmodisch*
on the dole	*stempeln gehen*
once	*einmal*
open	*draußen*
opinion	*Meinung, Ansicht*
opposite	*gegenüber, entgegengesetzt; das Gegenteil*
opposition	*Widerstand*
order	*Auftrag*
ordinary	*gewöhnlich*
organisation	*Organisation*
(to) organize	*organisieren*
origin	*Ursprung*
original	*original*
ours	*unsere(r, s)*
ourselves	*uns*
out of work	*arbeitslos*

outdoor	*im Freien*
outside	*außen, außerhalb*
over	*über*
(to) own	*besitzen*
owner	*Besitzer*
pack	*Bündel*
paper	*Papier*
(to) park	*parken (Auto)*
part	*Teil*
party	*Partei*
(to) pass	*vorbeigehen (an)*
password	*Parole, Passwort*
past	*vorüber, vorbei*
path	*Weg*
pay	*Bezahlung; bezahlen*
peace	*Friede*
peaceful	*friedlich*
pen	*Feder, Füller*
pencil	*Bleistift*
perfect	*vollkommen*
perhaps	*vielleicht*
(to) persuade	*überzeugen, überreden*
pet	*Haustier*
petrol	*Benzin*
(to) phone	*anrufen*
physical	*körperlich*
physical science	*Naturwissenschaft*
(to) pick	*(Früchte) pflücken; etw. abholen, aufheben*
picture	*Bild*
piece	*Stück*
pill	*Tablette*
pilot	*Pilot*
pity	*Mitleid*
plane	*Flugzeug; Fläche, Ebene*
planet	*Planet*
plant	*Pflanze*
plant	*Fabrikanlage, Werk*
plate	*Teller*
platform	*Bahnsteig; (Wahl-) Programm*
(to) play	*spielen*
pleasant	*angenehm*
(to) please	*jmdm. gefallen*
pleased	*zufrieden*
pleasure	*Vergnügen*
pocket	*Tasche*
poem	*Gedicht*
(to) point	*zeigen, deuten (auf)*
point	*Spitze*

police	*Polizei*
(to) polish	*polieren*
polite	*höflich*
political	*politisch*
politician	*Politiker*
politics	*Politik*
(to) pollute	*verschmutzen*
pollution	*(Umwelt-) Verschmutzung*
popular	*beliebt*
population	*Bevölkerung*
port	*Hafen (-stadt)*
position	*Stellung, Lage*
positive	*sicher, bestimmt*
possibility	*Möglichkeit*
possible	*möglich*
(to) post	*auf die Post geben*
pot	*Kanne, Topf*
potato	*Kartoffel*
(to) pour	*gießen*
power	*Kraft, Stärke*
powerful	*mächtig*
practice	*Übung*
(to) practise	*üben*
(to) prefer	*(etw.) vorziehen*
preparation	*Vorbereitung*
(to) prepare	*vorbereiten*
(to) present	*überreichen, schenken*
present	*gegenwärtig, momentan*
pretty	*hübsch; ziemlich*
price	*(Bezahl-) Preis*
pride	*Stolz*
(to) print	*drucken*
prison	*Gefängnis*
prize	*Preis (= Gewinn), Auszeichnung*
(to) produce	*herstellen*
production	*Herstellung*
profit	*Gewinn*
promise	*Versprechen; versprechen*
(to) protect	*(be-) schützen*
(to) protest	*protestieren*
proud	*stolz*
public	*öffentlich*
public transport	*öffentliche Verkehrsmittel*
pupil	*Schüler(in)*
pure	*rein, pur*
(to) push	*schieben, stoßen*
(to) put	*legen, stellen*
quarter	*Viertel*

quiet	*still, ruhig*
quite	*ganz, ziemlich*
race	*Rasse*
railway	*Eisenbahn, Gleise*
rain	*Regen*
rat	*Ratte*
rather	*lieber, ziemlich*
(to) react	*reagieren*
reaction	*Reaktion*
(to) read	*lesen*
ready	*fertig, bereit*
real	*wirklich, real*
really	*unbedingt, wirklich*
reason	*Grund, Anlass*
receptionist	*Empfangsdame /-chef (im Hotel)*
(to) record	*aufzeichnen, aufnehmen*
region	*Region, Bezirk, Bereich*
regular	*regelmäßig*
relative	*Verwandte(r)*
(to) remark	*äußern, bemerken*
(to) remember	*sich erinnern, denken an*
(to) remind (of)	*jmdn. erinnern (an)*
(to) rent	*mieten, leihen*
(to) repair	*reparieren*
report	*Bericht*
(to) reserve	*reservieren, zurückhalten, aufheben*
respect	*Hinsicht; Achtung*
rest	*Ruhepause; Rest*
result	*Ergebnis; Note*
(to) return	*zurückkehren; zurücksenden, -bringen*
revision exercise	*Wiederholungsübung*
right	*richtig, direkt; gerade; rechts*
(to) ring	*klingeln*
(to) rise	*(an-, auf-) steigen; aufgehen (Sonne)*
road	*Straße*
roll	*rollen*
romantic	*romantisch*
rope	*Seil, Tau*
rough	*rau, grob*
route	*Route, Strecke*
rubbish	*Mist, Müll*
rule	*Bestimmung, Verbot, Vorschrift*
(to) run	*laufen*
sad	*traurig, betrübt*

safety	*Sicherheit*
sail	*segeln, (mit dem Schiff) fahren, reisen*
salary	*Gehalt (Geld)*
sale	*Verkauf*
same	*der-, die-, dasselbe*
(to) save	*retten; aufbewahren*
(to) save	*sparen*
(to) saw	*sägen*
(to) say	*sagen*
scene	*Szene*
school lunch	*Mittagessen in der Schule*
science	*Naturwissenschaft*
(to) scream	*schreien*
screen	*Bildschirm*
sea	*das Meer, die See*
search	*Nachforschung, Suche; suchen*
season	*Jahreszeit*
secret	*Geheimnis*
(to) seem	*scheinen*
(to) sell	*verkaufen*
(to) send	*senden*
sentence	*Urteil (-sspruch)*
(to) separate [eit]	*trennen, (ab)teilen*
separate [it]	*getrennt, abgesondert*
serious	*ernst (-haft)*
(to) serve	*dienen*
(to) serve	*servieren*
service	*Bedienung; Dienst*
set	*Apparat, (Fernseh-); Satz*
(to) settle	*sich niederlassen; besiedeln*
(to) shine	*glänzen, scheinen*
(to) shock	*einen Schock versetzen*
(to) shoot	*schießen, erschießen*
should	*sollte*
(to) shout	*rufen, (an-) schreien*
shower	*Dusche*
(to) shut	*schließen*
shy	*schüchtern, scheu*
side	*Seite*
sight	*Anblick*
signal	*Signal*
(to) signal	*blinken*
simple	*einfach, schlicht*
since	*seit*
single	*einzeln; ledig*
sister	*Schwester*

(to) sit	*sitzen*
situation	*Lage, Situation*
size	*Größe*
skin	*Haut*
skirt	*Rock*
(to) slip	*ausrutschen und hinfallen*
slogan	*Werbespruch*
slow	*langsam*
smart	*schlau, clever, intelligent*
smell	*Geruch*
smoke	*Rauch*
snake	*Schlange*
snow	*Schnee*
so far	*bisher*
society	*Gesellschaft*
soft	*weich*
soft drink	*alkoholfreies Getränk*
(to) solve	*lösen, auflösen*
some	*einige, irgendein*
somebody	*jemand*
sometimes	*manchmal*
soon	*bald*
sore	*wund*
sorry	*es tut mir/ihr Leid*
sort	*Sorte*
sound	*Ton, Geräusch*
soup	*Suppe*
space	*Raum*
(to) speak	*sprechen, reden*
special	*besondere*
speech	*Rede*
speed	*Geschwindigkeit*
speed limit	*Geschwindigkeits-begrenzung*
(to) spell	*buchstabieren*
(to) spend	*(Zeit) verbringen; (Geld) ausgeben*
(to) split	*etwas teilen, halbieren*
(to) squash	*zerdrücken*
stadium	*Stadion*
(to) start	*anfangen, beginnen*
(to) steal	*stehlen*
still	*noch*
stomach	*Magen*
stone	*Stein*
(to) stop	*aufhören*
straight	*gerade*
strange	*fremdartig, seltsam*
(to) stress	*belasten, Stress*
(to) stretch	*sich erstrecken*

strict	*streng*
string	*Schnur*
strong	*stark*
stupid	*dumm, blöd*
subject	*Thema, Gegenstand, Schulfach*
subway	*U-Bahn*
success	*Erfolg*
such	*solche*
suddenly	*plötzlich, auf einmal*
(to) suggest	*vorschlagen*
suggestion	*Anregung, Vorschlag*
(to) suit	*passen*
suit	*(Herren-) Anzug, (Damen-) Kostüm*
(to) support	*ernähren; unterstützen*
sure	*natürlich*
(to) surprise	*überraschen*
surprise	*Überraschung*
sweet	*süß*
(to) swim	*schwimmen*
table	*Tisch*
(to) take part in	*teilnehmen an*
talent	*Begabung*
talk	*Gespräch*
tall	*hoch, groß*
(to) taste	*schmecken*
(to) teach	*unterrichten*
team	*Mannschaft*
(to) tear	*zerreißen, zerren*
technical	*technisch*
technology	*Technologie*
teeth	*Zähne*
telephone	*Telefon*
television	*Fernsehgerät*
temperature	*Temperatur*
tent	*Zelt*
terrible	*schrecklich*
test	*Prüfung*
than	*als (nach Komparativ)*
Thanksgiving	*amerikanisches Erntedankfest*
their	*ihr(e)*
theirs	*ihr(e, es)*
themselves	*sich*
theory	*Theorie*
thing	*Ding*
(to) think	*denken*
thirsty	*durstig*
though	*obwohl*
thought	*Gedanke*

thriller	*Reißer, Krimi*
through	*durch*
(to) throw	*werfen*
ticket	*Karte*
tidy	*ordentlich*
time	*Zeit*
timetable	*Fahrplan*
tip	*Trinkgeld*
together	*zusammen*
tonight	*heute Abend*
tool	*Werkzeug*
tooth	*Zahn*
top	*oberes Ende, Spitze*
(to) touch	*berühren*
tough	*zäh*
tourist	*Tourist*
towards	*in Richtung*
town	*Stadt*
toy	*Spielzeug*
track	*(Fuß-) Spur, Bahn*
trade	*Handel; Beruf*
tradition	*Überlieferung, Tradition*
traffic	*Verkehr*
traffic jam	*(Verkehrs-)Stau*
train	*Zug*
trainee	*Praktikant*
training	*Ausbildung*
transport	*Verkehrsmittel*
(to) travel	*reisen*
(to) trick	*jmdm. einen Streich spielen*
trouble	*Problem, Schwierigkeit*
true	*wahr*
(to) trust	*vertrauen*
(to) try	*versuchen*
(to) turn	*drehen*
twice	*zweimal*
typical (of)	*typisch (für)*
uncomfortable	*unbequem*
under	*unter*
(to) understand	*verstehen, begreifen*
unemployed	*arbeitslos*
unemployment	*Arbeitslosigkeit*
unfair	*ungerecht, unlauter*
unfriendly	*unfreundlich*
unhappy	*unglücklich*
unit	*Lektion, Einheit*
(to) unite	*(sich) vereinigen*
unknown	*unbekannt, nicht bekannt*

(to) unpack	*auspacken*
unpopular	*unbeliebt*
untidy	*unordentlich*
until	*bis*
upset	*aufgebracht, aufgeregt*
(to) use	*gebrauchen, nutzen*
useful	*nützlich*
useless	*nutzlos*
usual	*gewöhnlich*
van	*Transporter*
vandalism	*Zerstörungswut*
vegetable	*Gemüse*
vegetarian	*Vegetarier*
vehicle	*Fahrzeug*
victory	*Sieg*
view	*Ansicht, Meinung; Aussicht*
violence	*Gewalt, Gewalttätigkeit*
violent	*gewalttätig; heftig*
virtual	*so gut wie; nicht wirklich vorhanden*
vision	*Sehvermögen; Vorstellung*
(to) visit	*besuchen*
visitor	*Besucher*
voice	*Stimme*
volleyball	*Volleyball*
(to) vote	*abstimmen; wählen*
wage	*Lohn*
wallet	*Brieftasche*
war	*Krieg*
(to) wash	*waschen*
waste	*Abfall, Vergeudung, Verlust; verschwenden*
waste water	*Abwasser*
(to) watch	*sehen, fernsehen*
(to) wave	*winken*
wave	*Welle*
weak	*schwach*
weapon	*Waffe*
(to) wear	*tragen (Kleid, Uniform)*
weather	*Wetter*
weekday	*Wochentag*
weekend	*Wochenende*
(to) weigh	*wiegen*
weight	*Gewicht*
welcome	*willkommen*
well	*Ölquelle*
wet	*nass*
wheel	*Rad*

where	*wo*
while	*während*
(to) whisper	*flüstern*
whole	*ganz*
wholly	*gänzlich*
wide	*breit*
wife	*Ehefrau*
wing	*Flügel*
(to) wish	*wünschen*
without	*ohne*
woman	*Frau*
wood	*Holz*
word	*Wort*
working hours	*Arbeitszeit, Arbeitsstunden*
worried	*beunruhigt, besorgt*
(to) worry about	*sich Sorgen machen über*
worse	*schlechter, schlimmer*
worst	*der/die/das schlechteste*
worth	*wert (sein)*
wound [u:]	*Wunde*
wrong	*Unrecht; falsch, unrecht*
year	*Jahr*
yesterday	*gestern*
young	*jung*
yours	*deine(r, s), Ihre(r, s)*
yourself	*dich*
youth	*Jugendlicher; Jugend*
(to) zap	*hin- und herschalten*
zero	*Null*
zoo	*Tierpark, Zoo*

Countries – People – Languages

Country	Inhabitant	Language
Australia	Australian	English
Austria	Austrian	German
Belgium	Belgian	Flemish / French
Brazil	Brazilian	Portuguese
Britain	Briton	English
Canada	Canadian	English / French
Caribbean	Caribbean	English / Spanish
Denmark	Dane	Danish
England	Englishman	English
Finland	Fin	Finnish / Swedish
France	Frenchman	French
Germany	German	German
Greece	Greek	Greek
Holland/ Netherlands	Dutchman	Dutch
Hungary	Hungarian	Hungarian
India	Indian	Hindi / English
Ireland	Irishman	English / Gaelic
Italy	Italian	Italian
Japan	Japanese	Japanese
Mexico	Mexican	Spanish
Norway	Norwegian	Norwegian
New Zealand	New Zealander	English

Country	Inhabitant	Language
Poland	Pole	Polish
Portugal	Portuguese	Portuguese
Russia	Russian	Russian
Scotland	Scotsman	English / Gaelic
South Africa	South African	English / Afrikaans
Spain	Spaniard	Spanish
Sweden	Swede	Swedish
Switzerland	Swiss	German / French / Italian
Turkey	Turk	Turkish
United Kingdom	Briton	English
USA	American	English
Wales	Welshman	English / Gaelic

False Friends

alle Tage	every day	all day	*den ganzen Tag*
also	so, therefore	also	*auch, außerdem*
Argument	point	argument	*Wortwechsel, Streit*
Art	kind, sort, type	art	*(bildende) Kunst*
bald	soon	bald	*glatzköpfig, kahl*
bekommen	to receive, to get	to become	*werden*
Brief	letter	brief	*kurz, knapp*
Chef	boss	chef	*(Chef)koch, Köchin*
City	downtown, city centre	city	*Stadt*
delikat	delicious	delicate	*empfindlich, zerbrechlich*
Direktion	management	direction	*Richtung*
Distanz	reserve, coldness	distance	*Entfernung*
Dom	cathedral	dome	*Kuppel(dach)*
Dose	box, can, tin	dose	*Dosis*
eventuell	possible	eventual	*endlich, schließlich*
Fabrik	factory	fabric	*Stoff, Gewebe*
Fantasie	imagination	fantasy	*Vorstellung, Tagtraum*
fast	nearly, almost	fast	*schnell*
Fleisch	meat	flesh	*menschlicher Körper*
Formular	form	formula	*Formel*
Fotograf	photographer	photograph	*Fotografie*
Garage	garage (of a house)	garage	*Tankstelle, Autowerkstatt*
Handy	mobile phone	handy	*praktisch, nützlich*
Hochschule	college, university	high school	*Gymnasium, Oberschule*

Kanne	pot, kettle	can	*Dose*
komfortabel	luxurious	comfortable	*behaglich, bequem*
komisch	strange	comic(al)	*lustig*
Kritik	criticism	critic	*Kritiker*
Mappe	folder, file	map	*Landkarte*
Marmelade	jam	marmalade	*Orangenmarmelade*
Meinung	opinion	meaning	*Bedeutung, Sinn*
Menü	set meal, daily special	menu	*Speisekarte*
Mist	dung	mist	*Nebel*
ordinär	vulgar	ordinary	*alltäglich, gewöhnlich*
Preis	price	prize	*Siegerpreis*
Prospekt	folder, prospectus	prospect	*Aussicht*
raffiniert	clever	refined	*verfeinert, gebildet*
Rat	advice	rat	*Ratte*
Rente	pension	rent	*Miete*
Rezept	recipe	receipt	*Quittung*
seriös	respectable	serious	*ernsthaft*
sich blamieren	to embarrass	to blame	*jmdn. beschuldigen*
spenden	to donate sth.	to spend	*ausgeben*
Stadium	level	stadium	*Stadium*
Unternehmer	business person, employer	undertaker	*Leichenbestatter*
Warenhaus (Kaufhaus)	department store	warehouse	*Lagerhalle*

Unregelmäßige Verben

Infinitive	Past Tense	Past Participle	deutsche Übersetzung
be	was	been	*sein*
bear	bore	born(e)	*(er)tragen; gebären*
beat	beat	beaten	*schlagen*
begin	began	begun	*beginnen*
bet	bet	bet	*wetten*
blow	blew	blown	*blasen*
break	broke	broken	*brechen*
bring	brought	brought	*bringen*
build	built	built	*bauen*
burn	burnt/ed	burnt/ed	*brennen*
burst	burst	burst	*platzen*
buy	bought	bought	*kaufen*
catch	caught	caught	*fangen*
choose	chose	chosen	*wählen*
come	came	come	*kommen*
cost	cost	cost	*kosten*
cut	cut	cut	*schneiden*
do	did	done	*tun*
draw	drew	drawn	*zeichnen, ziehen*
dream	dreamt/ed	dreamt/ed	*träumen*
drink	drank	drunk	*trinken*
drive	drove	driven	*fahren*

Infinitive	Past Tense	Past Participle	deutsche Übersetzung
eat	ate	eaten	*essen*
fall	fell	fallen	*fallen*
feed	fed	fed	*füttern*
feel	felt	felt	*fühlen*
fight	fought	fought	*kämpfen*
find	found	found	*finden*
fly	flew	flown	*fliegen*
forget	forgot	forgotten	*vergessen*
get	got	got	*bekommen*
give	gave	given	*geben*
go	went	gone	*gehen*
grow	grew	grown	*wachsen*
hang	hung	hung	*hängen*
have	had	had	*haben*
hear	heard	heard	*hören*
hit	hit	hit	*treffen, schlagen*
hold	held	held	*halten*
hurt	hurt	hurt	*verletzen*
keep	kept	kept	*halten*
know	knew	known	*wissen*
lay	laid	laid	*legen*
lead	led	led	*leiten*
learn	learnt/ed	learnt/ed	*lernen*
leave	left	left	*lassen*
lend	lent	lent	*leihen*

Infinitive	Past Tense	Past Participle	deutsche Übersetzung
lean	leant/ed	leant/ed	*lehnen*
let	let	let	*lassen*
lie	lay	lain	*liegen*
light	lit/ed	lit/ed	*beleuchten*
lose	lost	lost	*verlieren*
make	made	made	*machen*
mean	meant	meant	*meinen, bedeuten*
meet	met	met	*treffen*
pay	paid	paid	*bezahlen*
put	put	put	*setzen, stellen, legen*
read [iː]	read [e]	read [e]	*lesen*
ride	rode	ridden	*fahren, reiten*
ring	rang	rung	*läuten*
rise	rose	risen	*aufstehen, aufgehen*
run	ran	run	*laufen, rennen*
say	said	said	*sagen*
see	saw	seen	*sehen*
seek	sought	sought	*suchen*
sell	sold	sold	*verkaufen*
send	sent	sent	*senden*
set	set	set	*setzen, stellen*
shake	shook	shaken	*schütteln*
shine	shone	shone	*scheinen*
shoot	shot	shot	*schießen*
show	showed	shown	*zeigen*

Infinitive	Past Tense	Past Participle	deutsche Übersetzung
shut	shut	shut	*schließen*
sing	sang	sung	*singen*
sit	sat	sat	*sitzen*
sleep	slept	slept	*schlafen*
smell	smelt	smelt	*riechen*
speak	spoke	spoken	*sprechen*
spell	spelt	spelt	*buchstabieren*
spend	spent	spent	*verbringen, ausgeben*
split	split	split	*spalten, teilen*
spring	sprang	sprung	*springen*
stand	stood	stood	*stehen*
steal	stole	stolen	*stehlen*
swim	swam	swum	*schwimmen*
swing	swung	swung	*schwingen*
take	took	taken	*nehmen*
teach	taught	taught	*lehren*
tear	tore	torn	*reißen*
tell	told	told	*erzählen*
think	thought	thought	*denken, glauben*
throw	threw	thrown	*werfen*
understand	understood	understood	*verstehen*
wake	woke	woken	*aufwachen, wecken*
wear	wore	worn	*tragen*
win	won	won	*gewinnen*
write	wrote	written	*schreiben*

Ihre Meinung ist uns wichtig!

Ihre Anregungen sind uns immer willkommen. Bitte informieren Sie uns mit diesem Schein über Ihre Verbesserungsvorschläge!

Titel-Nr.	Seite	Vorschlag

Bitte hier abtrennen

Bitte hier abtrennen

Zutreffendes bitte ankreuzen! Die Absenderin/der Absender ist:

- ☐ Lehrer/in in den Klassenstufen: ______
- ☐ Fachbetreuer/in
  Fächer: ______
- ☐ Seminarlehrer/in
  Fächer: ______
- ☐ Regierungsfachberater/in
  Fächer: ______
- ☐ Oberstufenbetreuer/in
- ☐ Schulleiter/in
- ☐ Referendar/in, Termin 2. Staatsexamen: ______
- ☐ Leiter/in Lehrerbibliothek
- ☐ Leiter/in Schülerbibliothek
- ☐ Sekretariat
- ☐ Eltern
- ☐ Schüler/in, Klasse: ______
- ☐ Sonstiges: ______

STARK Verlag
Postfach 1852
85318 Freising

20-VTX

Bitte ausfüllen und im frankierten Umschlag an uns einsenden. Für Fensterkuverts geeignet.

Kennen Sie Ihre Kundennummer? Bitte hier eintragen.

Absender (Bitte in Druckbuchstaben!)

Name/Vorname

Straße/Nr.

PLZ/Ort/Ortsteil

Telefon privat

Geburtsjahr

E-Mail

Schule/Schulstempel (Bitte immer angeben!)

Unterrichtsfächer: (Bei Lehrkräften!)

(Bitte blättern Sie um)

Abschluss-Prüfungsaufgaben

Mit vielen Jahrgängen der zentral gestellten Prüfungsaufgaben für den Hauptschulabschluss, einschließlich des aktuellen Jahrgangs. Zu allen Aufgaben vollständige, schülergerechte Lösungen.

Hauptschulabschluss Baden-Württemberg

Abschlussprüfungen im Format A4

Mit Lösungen im separaten Lösungsheft A5

Abschlussprüfung Mathematik	Best.-Nr. 83502
Lösungsheft zu Best.-Nr. 83502	Best.-Nr. 83505
Abschlussprüfung Deutsch	Best.-Nr. 83541
Abschlussprüf. Englisch mit MP3-CD	Best.-Nr. 83556
Sammelband Abschlussprüf. M, D, E	Best.-Nr. 83403
Lösungsheft zu Best.-Nr. 83403	Best.-Nr. 83404
Sammelband Abschlussprüfung M, D, E Werkrealschule Klasse 10	Best.-Nr. 83410

Quali/Hauptschulabschluss Bayern

Training Quali im Format A4

Mit Lösungen im separaten Lösungsheft A5

Training Quali Mathematik	Best.-Nr. 93503
Lösungsheft zu Best.-Nr. 93503	Best.-Nr. 93504
Training Quali Deutsch mit MP3-CD	Best.-Nr. 93545
Lösungsheft zu Best.-Nr. 93545	Best.-Nr. 93544
Training Quali Englisch mit MP3-CD	Best.-Nr. 93555
Lösungsheft zu Best.-Nr. 93555	Best.-Nr. 93554
Sammelband Training Quali M, D, E	Best.-Nr. 93413
Lösungsheft zu Best.-Nr. 93413	Best.-Nr. 93414

Quali im Format A5 mit Lösungen

Quali Mathematik	Best.-Nr. 93500
Quali Deutsch	Best.-Nr. 93540
Quali Englisch	Best.-Nr. 93550
Sammelband Quali M, D, E	Best.-Nr. 93400

Hauptschulabschluss 10. Klasse im Format A4 mit Lösungen

Abschlussprüfung Mathematik 10. Kl.	Best.-Nr. 93501
Abschlussprüfung Deutsch mit MP3-CD 10. Klasse	Best.-Nr. 93541
Abschlussprüfung Englisch mit MP3-CD 10. Klasse	Best.-Nr. 93551
Sammelband Abschlussprüfung Mathematik, Deutsch, Englisch 10. Klasse	Best.-Nr. 93410

Hauptschulabschluss Sachsen

Qualifizierender Hauptschulabschluss Mathematik, Deutsch Mittelschule Sachsen	Best.-Nr. 143410

Hauptschulabschluss Sachsen-Anhalt

Qualifizierter Hauptschulabschluss Mathematik, Deutsch Sekundarschule Sachsen-Anhalt	Best.-Nr. 153410

Hauptschulabschluss Thüringen

Qualifizierender Hauptschulabschluss Mathematik, Deutsch Regelschule Thüringen	Best.-Nr. 163410

Training Hauptschule Niedersachsen A4

Training Mathematik 9. Klasse	Best.-Nr. 33500
Training Mathematik 10. Klasse	Best.-Nr. 33501
Training Deutsch mit MP3-CD 9./10. Klasse	Best.-Nr. 33540
Training Englisch mit MP3-CD	Best.-Nr. 33550

Hauptschule Niedersachsen A5 NEU

Abschlussprüfung Mathematik 9. Kl.	Best.-Nr. 335001
Abschlussprüfung Mathematik 10. Kl.	Best.-Nr. 335011
Abschlussprüfung Deutsch 9. Klasse mit MP3-CD	Best.-Nr. 335401
Abschlussprüfung Deutsch 10. Klasse mit MP3-CD	Best.-Nr. 335411
Abschlussprüfung Englisch mit MP3-CD	Best.-Nr. 335501

Training Hauptschule Typ A NRW

Zentrale Prüfung Mathematik 10. Kl.	Best.-Nr. 53500
Zentrale Prüfung Deutsch 10. Klasse	Best.-Nr. 53540
Zentrale Prüfung Englisch mit MP3-CD 10. Klasse	Best.-Nr. 53550

Hauptschule NRW A5 NEU

Zentrale Prüfung Mathematik 10. Klasse	Best.-Nr. 535001
Zentrale Prüfung Deutsch 10. Klasse	Best.-Nr. 535401
Zentrale Prüfung Englisch 10. Klasse mit MP3-CD	Best.-Nr. 535501

Hauptschule Hessen

Mit Lösungen im separaten Lösungsheft A5

Abschlussprüfung Mathematik	Best.-Nr. 63500
Lösungsheft zu Best.-Nr. 63500	Best.-Nr. 63504
Abschlussprüfung Deutsch	Best.-Nr. 63540
Lösungsheft zu Best.-Nr. 63540	Best.-Nr. 63544
Abschlussprüfung Englisch	Best.-Nr. 63550
Abschlussprüfung Englisch Mit Hörverstehenstexten auf MP3-CD	Best.-Nr. 63555
Lösungsheft zu Best.-Nr. 63550/63555	Best.-Nr. 63554
Sammelband Abschlussprüf. M, D, E	Best.-Nr. 63400
Lösungsheft zu Best.-Nr. 63400	Best.-Nr. 63401

Bestellungen bitte direkt an:
STARK Verlagsgesellschaft mbH & Co. KG · Postfach 1852 · D-85318 Freising
Telefon 0180 3 179000* · Telefax 0180 3 179001*
www.stark-verlag.de · info@stark-verlag.de
*9 Cent pro Min. aus dem deutschen Festnetz, Mobilfunk bis 42 Cent pro Min.
Aus dem Mobilfunknetz wählen Sie die Festnetznummer: 08167 9573-0

Lernen · Wissen · Zukunft
STARK

20-VTX